DAILY SUMMER ACTIVITIES

BETWEEN GRADES 4 AND 5

D1308486

Algonquin Area Public Library
2600 Harnish Dr.
Algonquin, IL 60102
www.aapld.org

Writing: Jill Norris
Content Editing: Marilyn Evans
Copy Editing: Cathy Harber
Art Direction: Cheryl Puckett
Cover Design: Liliana Potigian
Illustration: Jo Larsen
Design/Production: Cheryl Puckett

EMC 1031

Evan-Moor
EDUCATIONAL PUBLISHERS®
Helping Children Learn since 1979

Visit
teaching-standards.com
to view a correlation
of this book.
This is a free service.

**Correlated to State and
Common Core State Standards**

**Congratulations on your purchase of some of the
finest teaching materials in the world.**

*No part of this book may be reproduced
in any form or stored in any retrieval system
without the written permission of publisher.*

For information about other Evan-Moor products, call 1-800-777-4362,
fax 1-800-777-4332, or visit our Web site, www.evan-moor.com.
Entire contents © 2005 EVAN-MOOR CORP.
18 Lower Ragsdale Drive, Monterey, CA 93940-5746. Printed in USA.

Contents

Skills

Skills	Week 1	2	3	4	5	6	7	8	9	10
Reading Comprehension										
Nonfiction	●	●		●	●	●	●		●	●
Fiction	●		●	●	●			●	●	
Make Connections	●	●	●	●	●	●	●	●	●	●
Sequencing Events					●					
Main Idea and Details	●		●			●	●	●	●	
Character and Setting			●			●	●			●
Compare/Contrast		●	●			●	●		●	●
Inference	●	●	●					●	●	●
Context Clues	●	●	●	●			●		●	●
Grammar/Usage/Mechanics										
Phonics	●		●	●			●	●		
Spelling	●	●	●	●	●	●	●	●	●	●
Alphabetical Order	●									
Contractions	●		●			●				
Possessives				●	●			●		
Singular/Plural			●	●	●					
Parts of Speech	●	●	●	●	●	●		●	●	●
Conjunctions			●							
Subject/Verb Agreement	●	●	●	●			●	●	●	●
Abbreviations	●						●			
Capitalization	●	●	●	●	●	●	●	●	●	●
Punctuation	●	●	●	●	●	●	●	●	●	●
Verb Tenses	●	●		●						
Compound Sentences	●	●								
Idioms		●								
Quotation Marks		●		●	●	●	●		●	
Syllabification						●				
Vocabulary Development										
Rhyming Words		●								
Silent Letters				●			●			
Compound Words			●			●				
Comparatives/Superlatives						●				
Homophones/Homographs		●				●		●		
Writing										
Write a Sentence	●	●	●	●	●	●	●	●	●	●
Write a Paragraph	●	●	●					●	●	●
Write a List				●	●				●	
Journal Writing	●	●	●	●	●	●	●	●	●	●
Write Questions										●

©2005 by Evan-Moor Corp. • Daily Summer Activities 4–5 • EMC 1031

Skills	Week									
	1	2	3	4	5	6	7	8	9	10
Handwriting										
Cursive Writing Practice	●	●	●	●	●	●	●	●	●	●
Math										
Sequencing				●						
Patterning					●					
Number Words				●						
Word Problems	●	●	●	●	●	●	●	●	●	●
Money	●	●	●		●		●	●	●	●
Place Value	●				●					
Column Addition/Subtraction	●	●			●	●				
Addition	●	●			●	●	●			●
Subtraction	●	●			●	●	●			
Borrowing		●			●	●	●			
Carrying	●	●			●	●	●			
Multiplication	●	●	●		●			●	●	●
Division				●	●	●	●			
Graphs/Grids/Charts	●	●	●	●		●		●	●	
Fractions	●				●		●			
Measurement		●	●	●			●		●	
Tell Time			●	●	●		●	●		●
Shapes/Angles					●		●	●		●
Perimeter/Area			●				●			
Common Factors										●
Mean/Median/Range					●					
Pre-Algebra								●	●	
Ratios	●									
Geography										
Map-Reading Skills	●		●	●	●		●	●	●	●
Political Maps				●	●		●			●
Physical Maps								●		
Road Maps									●	
Globes	●	●								
Legends		●		●					●	
Compass Rose/Directions		●							●	●
Scales					●					
Latitude and Longitude					●					
Grids					●					
Population						●				
Thinking Skills										
Riddles/Problem Solving	●	●	●	●	●	●	●	●	●	●

About This Book

What's in It

Ten Weekly Sections

Each section contains half-page and full-page activities that help children learn reading, writing, math, geography, spelling, grammar, and critical-thinking skills.

Each week, your child will work on the following:

Reading	▶ comprehension activities on fiction and nonfiction reading passages
Spell It!	▶ an activity to practice the week's spelling words
Write It Right	▶ an editing activity to correct errors in spelling, grammar, and punctuation
Handwriting	▶ a writing activity to practice penmanship skills
Language Lines	▶ activities that practice language skills, including compound words, parts of speech, subject/verb agreement, and quotation marks
Math Time	▶ activities that practice math skills, including computation, basic geometry, and pre-algebra
In My Own Words	▶ creative-writing exercises
Geography	▶ a map activity that tests basic geography concepts
Problem Solving	▶ a critical-thinking activity
What Happened Today?	▶ a place to record a memorable moment from the week, and a reading log to record the number of minutes spent reading each day

©2005 by Evan-Moor Corp. • Daily Summer Activities 4–5 • EMC 1031

How to Use It

The short practice lessons in *Daily Summer Activities* prepare your child for the coming school year by making sure that he or she remembers all of the skills and concepts learned in fourth grade. After completing the activities in this book, your child will feel more confident as he or she begins the new school year. You can help your child by following the suggestions below.

▶ Provide Time and Space

Make sure that your child has a quiet place for completing the activities. The practice session should be short and positive. Consider your child's personality and other activities as you decide how and where to schedule daily practice periods.

▶ Encourage and Support

Your response is important to your child's feelings of success. Keep your remarks positive and recognize the effort your child has made. Work through challenging activities and correct mistakes together.

▶ Check in Each Week

Use the weekly record sheet to talk about the most memorable moments and learning experiences of the week and to discuss the books your child is reading.

▶ Be a Model Reader

The most important thing you can do is to make sure your child sees you reading. Read books, magazines, and newspapers. Visit libraries and bookstores. Point out interesting signs, maps, and advertisements wherever you go. Even though your child is an independent reader, you can still share the reading experience by discussing what you read every day.

▶ Go on Learning Excursions

Learning takes place everywhere and through many experiences. Build learning power over the summer by:

- visiting local museums and historic sites. Use a guidebook or search online to find points of interest in your area.

- collecting art materials and working together to create a collage, mobile, or scrapbook.

- going to a play, concert, or other show at a local theater or performance center.

- planting a garden. If you are short on space, plant in containers.

- creating a movie of your child's favorite story. Write a simple script and make basic costumes and props, and recruit friends and family members to be actors. Practice until everyone is comfortable before shooting the video.

Spell It! This list contains all of the weekly spelling words practiced in the book.

A

afternoon
agree
alphabet
although
among
anybody
aren't

B

basketball
become
believe
bought
breakfast
busiest
butterfly

C

chews
chief
choose
classroom
climb
clue
cough
country
cousin

D

danger
deceive
describe
destroy
disappoint
doctor
due

E

earthquake
enough
everybody
everywhere

F

favorite
fearful
flashlight
future

G

gnat
gnaw

H

half
happiest
happiness
harmful
haven't
headache
height
homework
hour

K

kindest
knight
knot
knowledge

L

largest
learn
lifeguard
limb
loyal

M

maybe
menu
might
minute
myself

N

neighbor
nephew
news
niece
noise

O

o'clock
often
our
outside

P

peace
photograph
piece
purchase

Q

quarter
quickly
quietly

R

received
refuse
right

S

secondhand
several
shoelace
skyscraper
smartest
something
sure
sweatshirt

T

they're
thirsty
thoughtless
threw
through
together
triangle
tried
trouble
truth

U

unknown
used
useless

V

variety
voice
voyage

W

wait
weight
which
whole
whose
without
world
worthless
wouldn't
wristwatch
write
written
wrong

Y

you're

©2005 by Evan-Moor Corp. • Daily Summer Activities 4–5 • EMC 1031

Color a for each page finished.

Parent's Initials

Monday	☆ ☆	_____
Tuesday	☆ ☆	_____
Wednesday	☆ ☆	_____
Thursday	☆ ☆	_____
Friday	☆ ☆	_____

Spelling Words

they're	world
wouldn't	doctor
aren't	learn
o'clock	thirsty
haven't	danger
you're	purchase

A Memorable Moment

What sticks in your mind about this week? Write about it.

_____

_____

_____

_____

Keeping Track

Color a book for every 15 minutes you read.

Monday	Tuesday	Wednesday	Thursday	Friday

Describe a character that you read about this week.

_____

_____

_____

_____

Introducing the Spotted Salamander

The spotted salamander remains almost unchanged from the first salamander that walked on the Earth about 330 million years ago. It lives in caves or under rocks and logs, and it only moves during the blackest hours of the night. It eats insects and worms and lives in the earthen darkness, just as its early ancestors did. Its soft legs, clawless toes, and moist body look just like those of generations of salamanders that have come before it.

Its eyes peer into the darkness, but they do not move like other creatures' eyes. The spotted salamander only sees things that move. It cannot see things that are still. It "hears" with primitive ears that lie inside its head and along its body and tail.

Once a year, on the night of the first spring rain after the first spring thaw, it visits the same woodland pond that its ancestors visited. There it lays its eggs. Then it returns to the darkness of its home in the moist earth of the forest.

1. What is the main idea of this article?

_____

2. List three supporting details that tell about the main idea.

_____

_____

_____

3. Underline the topic sentence in the first paragraph.

4. How are the eyes and ears of the spotted salamander different from most animals today?

_____

_____

_____

Write It Right

1. in april we will have cheerleading tryouts at lincoln junior high

_____

_____

2. tonya slip on the ice she fall on her write foot

_____

3. mrs jackson mrs ruiz and mr evans is in charge of the basketball team

_____

_____

MATH ⊙ TIME

Write the place value of the 4 in the numbers below.

4,093 _____

$14.92 _____

948 _____

74 _____

8.4 _____

42,081 _____

6.04 _____

4,982,000 _____

 **Spell It!** R controls many vowel sounds so that the vowel + r makes the sound you hear in her.

Underline the r-controlled vowel sounds in these words.

world   doctor   learn   thirsty   danger   purchase

Use the words above to complete these sentences.

1. There are many places in the _____ where people are

_____ because there is not enough water.

2. The _____ warned her patient about the _____ of

the operation.

3. It is important to _____ about the features of an automobile

before you _____ it.

Copy this riddle in your best handwriting. Then answer it.

Round and round the rugged rock
The ragged rascal ran.
How many Rs are there in that?
Now tell me if you can.

_____
_____
_____
_____
_____
_____

Answer:

Tuesday

Week 1

Language Lines

Write the words that have been combined to make each contraction.

they're _____ _____

wouldn't _____ _____

aren't _____ _____

haven't _____ _____

you're _____ _____

o'clock _____ _____ _____

MATH TIME

Find the answers.

34	29	46	83	91	52	77	90
+ 26	+ 45	+ 13	+ 74	+ 49	+ 28	+ 36	+ 88
61	37	85	27	76	16	98	14
+ 82	+ 29	+ 48	+ 19	+ 79	+ 46	+ 23	+ 37
94	16	69	37	21	48	80	55
+ 17	+ 89	+ 34	+ 81	+ 60	+ 78	+ 47	+ 68

Week 1   Tuesday

The Argument Sticks

An Iroquois Tale

Two brothers were arguing. Each thought that he was right. Each brother clenched his fist and shook it at the other.

Then the boys' mother gave them three sticks. She explained, "These sticks will solve your argument."

The mother walked into the woods with her sons. Each carried a stick. When they had gone a little way they stopped. "Now we set up the sticks," she said. She showed the boys how to lean the three sticks together so that they stood alone.

Then she said, "The sticks must be left for one month. If they fall over toward the north, the one who set up the stick on the north is right. If they fall over to the south, the one who set up the stick on the south is right." The boys were happy. They left the sticks in the woods and went home.

A month later the boys thought of the sticks. They went into the woods to find out who had been right. The sticks had fallen in a heap. They had begun to rot so they couldn't tell who the winner was. This did not trouble the brothers because they couldn't remember what the argument had been about in the first place.

1. What was the problem in this tale?

_____

2. Do you think the argument sticks helped to solve the brothers' problem in this tale? Tell why you think as you do.

_____

_____

3. Write one way you would solve a problem.

_____

_____

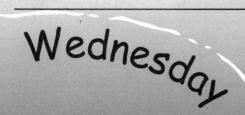

Wednesday

Week 1

15

Write a definition of the underlined word in each sentence. Use the context (the meaning of the sentence) to help you. Then check your definition with a dictionary.

1. The spotted salamander is active at night, so we call it <u>nocturnal</u>.

_____

2. The <u>descendents</u> of the first spotted salamander haven't changed significantly in over 300 million years.

_____

3. The spelunker <u>peered</u> up the crevice in the dim light.

_____

4. He knew it would be difficult to <u>traverse</u> the slick walls of the cave, but he needed to get to the other side.

_____

MATH TIME   Learn About Ratios

The numbers are a special comparison called a ratio.

Write how many shaded squares and how many white squares are in each line.

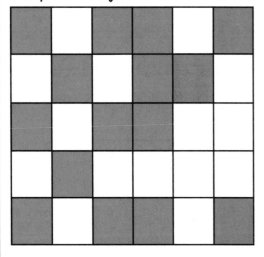

4 : 2

___ : ___

___ : ___

___ : ___

___ : ___

What is the ratio for the whole figure?

_____

Were you surprised at the overall ratio? Tell why or why not.

_____

_____

Geography

The globe can be divided in half two ways. Each half is called a hemisphere. When it is divided at the equator, the Southern and Northern Hemispheres are created. When it is divided along the prime meridian and 180° longitude, the Western and Eastern Hemispheres are created.

Use the drawings to identify the hemispheres in which you live. Then complete the sentences.

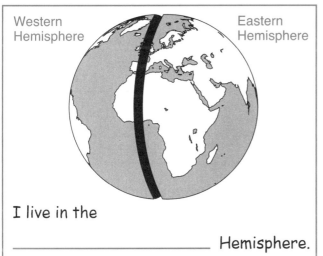

Western Hemisphere

Eastern Hemisphere

I live in the

_____ Hemisphere.

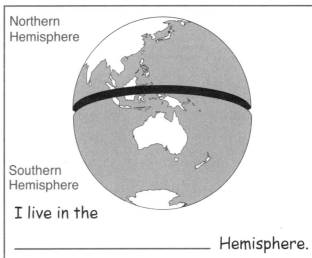

Northern Hemisphere

Southern Hemisphere

I live in the

_____ Hemisphere.

In My Own Words...

You are an astronaut looking back at Earth from space. Write an entry in your space log telling what you see.

_____

_____

_____

_____

_____

_____

Language Lines

A noun names a person, place, or thing.

Circle the nouns in the passage below.

Animals sleep in many different positions. Horses and giraffes sleep standing up. Bats sleep upside down. Hippos sleep in a big heap. I sleep in a comfortable, soft, cozy, warm bed.

Remember what you read.

Sleep Standing Up	Sleep Upside Down	Sleep in a Heap
_____	_____	_____
_____	_____	_____

MATH TIME

Tell what part of each figure is shaded.

1.

2.

3.

Are any of the shaded sections equivalent?

yes   no

_____

4.

5.

6.

Tell which ones.

_____

_____

Week 1   Thursday

Write these words in alphabetical order. **A B C**

turn, duck, whistle, eagle, Relax!, hawk, zip, juniper, lupine, Nice!, grouse, yell, maple, Perfect!, apples, Quiet!, falcon, ivy, Shush!, bananas, unpack, vote, cherries, Ouch!, kudzu

The list above can be divided into five categories.
Color the boxes in each category a different color.

MATH TIME

Find the answers.

1. Thomas is saving money to buy a game cartridge. The cartridge costs $24.95. If he has $12.50, how much more money does Thomas need? _____

2. Sally's dog had six puppies. If Sally keeps one puppy for herself and sells the others for $12 each, how much money will she earn? _____

3. Dave has five more chickens than he has dogs. He has one less cat than he has dogs. If he has three dogs, how many pets does he have? _____

Friday

Week 1

Whose Tree?

Each state in the United States has chosen a special tree to represent their state. Use the clues and the matrix to match the following states and their trees. Write yes to show a correct answer. Make an X to show incorrect answers.

- Rhode Island's tree is two words. The first letter of the first word for the state and the tree are the same.

- California's tree is named for the color of its trunk.

- The American elm is not the state tree of Florida, Nevada, or Georgia.

- Oregon's tree is a popular Christmas tree that begins with a person's name.

- The name of South Carolina's tree begins with the same letter as the state.

- The single-leaf piñon tree represents a state that borders California.

	redwood	single-leaf piñon	American elm	live oak	Douglas fir	Sabal palmetto	red maple
Oregon							
Massachusetts & N. Dakota							
Rhode Island							
California							
Florida & S. Carolina							
Nevada							
Georgia							

©2005 by Evan-Moor Corp. • Daily Summer Activities 4-5 • EMC 1031

Color a for each page finished.

Parent's Initials

Monday	☆	☆	_____
Tuesday	☆	☆	_____
Wednesday	☆	☆	_____
Thursday	☆	☆	_____
Friday	☆	☆	_____

Spelling Words

wait	right
weight	write
piece	choose
peace	chews
hour	threw
our	through

A Memorable Moment

What sticks in your mind about this week? Write about it.

_____

_____

_____

_____

Keeping Track

Color a book for every 15 minutes you read.

Monday	Tuesday	Wednesday	Thursday	Friday

Describe the setting of a story you read this week.

_____

_____

_____

©2005 by Evan-Moor Corp. • Daily Summer Activities 4–5 • EMC 1031

Jesse Owens

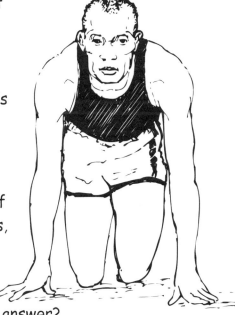

Jesse Owens was the son of Alabama sharecroppers. As a child, he was skinny and often sick. When he was nine, his family moved to Ohio to find a better life.

It was there, while Jesse was in junior high school, that he met his mentor, Charles Riley, a gym teacher and coach of the track team. Coach Riley taught Jesse to run and jump. Jesse worked hard. He set his first track and field record in that year. He ran the 100-yard dash in 10 seconds flat. He went on to set many records in high school and college.

At the 1936 Olympics in Berlin, Jesse won four gold medals as he set new world records in three events. One of the greatest track and field athletes of the United States, Jesse Owens began life as a poor, sickly boy and became a world hero.

1. If someone asked you who Jesse Owens was, what would you answer?

_____

_____

2. What are some of the obstacles Jesse overcame in his life?

_____

_____

3. A tag line often follows the title of a biography. Circle the tag line you think is best for this story.

   a. Poor Boy Makes Good   b. Running to a Better Life   c. The Difference a Coach Makes

4. What do you think young people could learn from Jesse Owens?

_____

_____

_____

Week 2

1. ben taked pictures of the team for boy's life magazine

_____

2. does you like a aluminum bat or an wooden one

_____

3. mom said we needs to stop to bye gas before we leave for bass lake

_____

_____

MATH TIME

Find the answers.

96	24	81	75	39	48	52	63	17	80
− 62	− 18	− 56	− 26	− 22	− 39	− 47	− 60	− 13	− 74

25	90	31	67	42	79	86	59	68	31
− 18	− 73	− 22	− 48	− 35	− 49	− 59	− 31	− 65	− 17

83	27	75	46	53	1 1	37	94	52	61
− 59	− 18	− 58	− 27	− 44	− 10	− 29	− 78	− 36	− 45

Spell It!

Homophones are words that sound the same but have different meanings.

Use homophone pairs from your spelling list to complete each pair of sentences.

1. She practices the violin for an _____ every afternoon.

   Mr. Jenkins lives next door to _____ house.

2. It is hard to _____ for your birthday to arrive.

   The clerk checks the _____ of the fruit to determine its price.

3. I have to go _____ the garden to get to the gate.

   My baby sister _____ the strained carrots on the floor.

4. A time without conflict is called _____ .

   Would you like a _____ of cherry pie?

Handwriting

Use write or right to complete the sentences. Then copy them in your best handwriting.

Could it be _____ to _____ with your _____?

Could it be _____ to _____ with your left?

I think that it's quite all _____

To _____ with your left or your _____!

©2005 by Evan-Moor Corp. • Daily Summer Activities 4-5 • EMC 1031

Write a or an in front of each noun below.

_____ armadillo   _____ mountain

_____ icicle   _____ dragonfly

_____ eagle   _____ garage

_____ zipper   _____ obstacle

a

an

Write a sentence that explains when you use a and when you use an in front of a noun.

_____

MATH TIME

Measure the lines in inches.

AB is _____.

BC is _____.

AC is _____.

AB + AC is longer than BC.

   yes   no

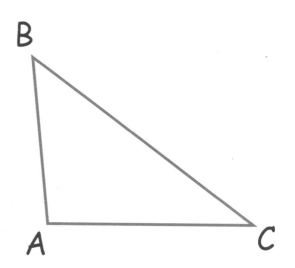

Draw a line the length of AB + AC + BC.

©2003 by Evan-Moor Corp. • Daily Summer Activities 4–5 • EMC 1031

The Hermit Crab

It hasn't a home of its own.
It uses a discarded shell.
Slipping into the emptiness
It's learned recycling well.

1. Describe the hermit crab's home.

_____

_____

2. What conservation guideline does the hermit crab follow?

☐ Reduce the amount of trash you produce.

☐ Reuse things that have been used before.

☑ Recycle materials to make something new.

An Orca

The orca flips and turns,
The gymnast of the seas.
It weighs four tons or more
But breaches with great ease.

1. What two things does the metaphor in this poem compare?

_____

2. Why is the orca's grace unusual?

_____

What rhyme pattern do the
two poems on this page follow?

Wednesday

Week 2

©2005 by Evan-Moor Corp. • Daily Summer Activities 4–5 • EMC 1031

1. A yard is a measurement of length. What else can the word yard mean?

_____

Write one sentence using the two different meanings of the word yard.

_____

_____

2. A key is a metal object used to turn the bolt of a lock.
   What does the word key mean in this sentence?

The map key indicates that the city has an airport.

_____

_____

MATH TIME

Find the answers.

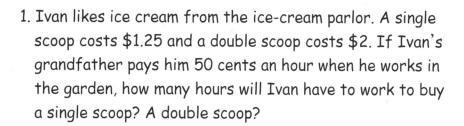

1. Ivan likes ice cream from the ice-cream parlor. A single
   scoop costs $1.25 and a double scoop costs $2. If Ivan's
   grandfather pays him 50 cents an hour when he works in
   the garden, how many hours will Ivan have to work to buy
   a single scoop? A double scoop?

   _____ single

   _____ double

2. Mr. Sweet can make 40 single-scoop cones from a
   five-gallon tub of ice cream. If the ice cream and the
   cones cost $28, what is Mr. Sweet's profit if he sells
   only single scoops?

   _____

 # Geography

Match the word with the phrase that tells what it means.

map   • a book of maps

globe   • a picture of a part of the Earth's surface

legend   • a symbol telling directions

compass rose   • a sphere with a map of the Earth on it

atlas   • an explanation of the symbols used on a map

In My Own Words...

Imagine your favorite kind of ice cream. You are standing outside the ice-cream store. It's a hot day and you have two dollars in your pocket. Describe what happens next.

_____

_____

_____

_____

_____

_____

_____

_____

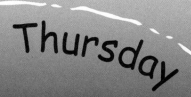

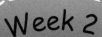

Tell what the underlined phrase in each sentence means.

1. Tommy is always <u>on the ball</u>.

_____

2. Johnny was <u>horsing around</u>.

_____

3. Mr. Jones's <u>bark is worse than his bite</u>.

_____

MATH◯TIME

Add or subtract.

356	782	978	320	507	401	823	649	105
+ 475	- 538	+ 827	- 186	+ 368	- 285	+ 794	- 470	+ 787

905	284	768	472	691	537	123	892	409
+ 157	- 135	+ 233	- 329	+ 409	- 185	+ 879	- 573	+ 607

Use pairs of rhyming words to answer the questions. You will find one-half of each pair in the word box.

Word Box

red	big	flat	green	lucky	marriage

1. What do you call someone whose hair is the color of a tomato? _____

2. What do you call a large hog? _____

3. What do you call a cap after an elephant sits on it? _____

4. What do you call a grass-colored vegetable? _____

5. What do you call a web-footed winner? _____

6. What do you call a wagon used by the bride and groom? _____

MATH TIME

Pete's Bugs

Pete collects bugs and keeps them in a cage. Once a week he opens the lid to add 5 new bugs. Each time he does, 3 bugs get away. If he starts with 18 bugs, how many bugs will he have at the end of six weeks? _____

Complete this table to find the answer to the question.

	WEEK 1	WEEK 2	WEEK 3	WEEK 4	WEEK 5	WEEK 6
Beginning of Week						
Bugs In						
Bugs Out						
End of Week						

Friday

Week 2

Magic Squares

Fill in each magic square. Use the numerals 1 through 9. Use each number only once per square. The numbers must total 15 when they are added together horizontally and vertically. Give three different solutions.

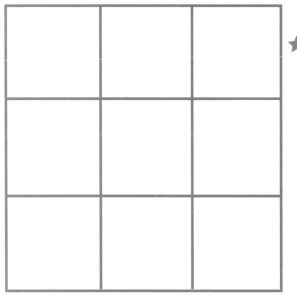

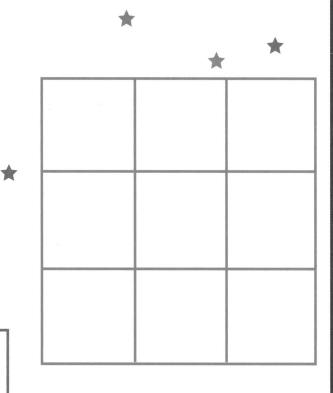

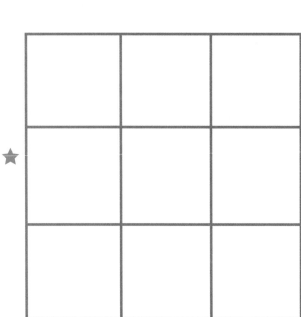

On another sheet of paper, create your own magic square puzzle.

Color a for each page finished.

Parent's Initials

Monday ☆ ☆ _____

Tuesday ☆ ☆ _____

Wednesday ☆ ☆ _____

Thursday ☆ ☆ _____

Friday ☆ ☆ _____

Spelling Words

breakfast   sweatshirt
earthquake   wristwatch
flashlight   afternoon
headache   everybody
lifeguard   everywhere
skyscraper   shoelace

A Memorable Moment

What sticks in your mind about this week? Write about it.

_____

_____

_____

_____

Keeping Track

Color a book for every 15 minutes you read.

Monday	Tuesday	Wednesday	Thursday	Friday

Think about the books you read this week. Tell about a character's problem and how it was solved.

_____

_____

_____

_____

Dear Anna,

   When you look outside your window and see the open spaces, it must be very different from when I look outside my window here in the city. You said that it seems like the prairie reaches out and touches the places where the sky comes down. At my house, all I can see from my windows are houses and streets. I can't see the horizon. It seems as if I could climb from roof to roof to reach the stars.

   What is it like at night at your house? There are millions of lights here in the city. It is never really quiet here. There are always noises—buzzes and beeps, honking and hollering. Is nighttime quiet at your house?

   I have a little brother just like yours, and it bugs me when he asks the same question over and over. I try to answer his questions, but sometimes I ask him a question instead of giving an answer. That can stop "the why cycle." Do you have the same problem? Do you have any better idea for solving it?

   Write back soon.

                                        Your pen pal,
                                        Harriet

1. What kind of place does Harriet live in?

_____

2. Where do you think Anna lives?

_____

3. What do the two girls have in common?

_____

_____

4. What is your house like at night? Write your reply as if Harriet had asked you.

_____

_____

1. morris leaved his job and moved to dallas texas to be a fire fighter

_____

_____

2. clarise antonio and margaret have went to tennis camp since they was seven

_____

_____

3. the scientists didnt gave up when they couldnt figure out the problem

_____

_____

MATH TIME

Give the perimeter and the area.

2

6

area _____

perimeter _____

5

3

area _____

perimeter _____

4

4

area _____

perimeter _____

©2005 by Evan-Moor Corp. • Daily Summer Activities 4–5 • EMC 1031

Spell It!

Write the words that combine to form each of the following words. Then write a sentence using the two words, explaining each compound word.

breakfast   break + fast

You break your nightlong fast **when you eat** breakfast.

1. earthquake _____ + _____

_____

2. headache _____ + _____

_____

3. lifeguard _____ + _____

_____

4. wristwatch _____ + _____

_____

Handwriting

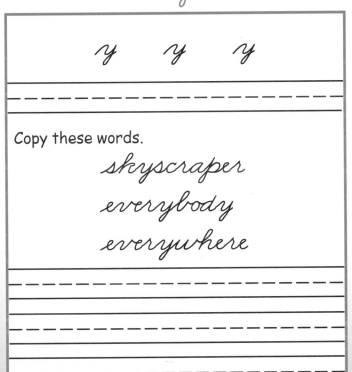

$\mathscr{Y}$ $\mathscr{y}$ $\mathscr{y}$

Copy these words.

skyscraper

everybody

everywhere

$\mathscr{Y}$ $\mathscr{Y}$ $\mathscr{Y}$

Copy these words.

Yolanda

Yesterday

Yemen

Tuesday

Week 3

Use conjunctions (and, but, or) to combine each pair of simple sentences into a compound sentence. Use a comma before each conjunction.

1. Aunt Carol baked cookies. The children ate them all.

   _____

   _____

2. The explorers searched the ice field. They never reached the South Pole.

   _____

   _____

3. There was a large crack in the bike path. I had to swerve to avoid it.

   _____

   _____

MATH TIME

Find the answers.

308	769	853	972	657	896
x 7	x 4	x 6	x 9	x 1	x 8
409	692	738	557	985	850
x 8	x 6	x 0	x 9	x 5	x 7

Week 3

Tuesday

©2005 by Evan-Moor Corp. • Daily Summer Activities 4–5 • EMC 1031

A Letter in the Mail

It was a crisp autumn morning, and I scuffled through the leaves on the sidewalk. The mailman waved as he drove off to his next stop. I waved back and paused in front of the bank of mailboxes. I took a deep breath and paused for a moment before I opened our box. Would this be the day? Would the letter finally come?

I turned the key in the lock and slowly swung the door open. On top of the usual flyers announcing the current price of chicken legs and apples and the biggest and best furniture sale were three letters. Would one of the letters have my name on it?

I blew on my fingers and rubbed the shiny penny in my pocket for good luck. I reached into the box and pulled out the letters. The letter on top was addressed to my mom. It was from the phone company, probably a bill. The next letter was handwritten and addressed to the family. It had to be from Grandma because nobody else ever wrote handwritten letters.

One more letter...I took a deep breath and looked at the return address. It was from Space Camp. It was addressed to me. This was the letter I had been waiting for! I gulped and felt the smooth, stiff envelope. Was the news inside good or bad? Had I won the scholarship?

I really wanted to go to Space Camp. I had spent hours working on the essay that accompanied the application. Mrs. Johnson had sent a great letter of recommendation. But I knew that lots of other fifth-graders were anxiously waiting, too. They all probably really wanted to go to Space Camp. They all had probably spent hours on their essays. Their teachers had probably written great letters of recommendation for them. My stomach fluttered and my mouth went dry.

What news was inside that envelope?

1. Was the character nervous about opening the letter? Tell how you know.

_____

2. What reasons did the character have for being excited about the contents of the Space Camp letter?

_____

3. What reasons did the character have for being worried about the contents?

_____

©2005 by Evan-Moor Corp. • Daily Summer Activities 4-5 • EMC 1031

Language Lines

A common noun names any person, place, thing, or idea.
A proper noun names a specific person, place, thing, or idea.
Proper nouns begin with capital letters.

Write a proper noun to name the following:

your whole name _____

your school _____

your town _____

a song _____

a movie _____

a mountain _____

MATH TIME

Find the answers.

34	57	82	76	83	79	61	95
x 8	x 7	x 5	x 9	x 4	x 6	x 2	x 3

87	29	45	68	53	31	76	99
x 3	x 8	x 9	x 4	x 6	x 2	x 7	x 5

70	93	37	89	64	56	28	19
x 6	x 8	x 7	x 5	x 9	x 6	x 4	x 8

©2005 by Evan-Moor Corp. • Daily Summer Activities 4–5 • EMC 1031

Geography

Antarctica Cross Section

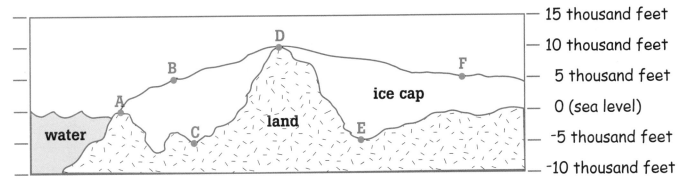

15 thousand feet
10 thousand feet
5 thousand feet
0 (sea level)
-5 thousand feet
-10 thousand feet

1. What is the approximate elevation of these points?

Point A _____   Point D _____

Point B _____   Point E _____

Point C _____   Point F _____

2. Do you know the elevation of the place where you live? If not, try to find out.

In My Own Words...

You have just received a letter congratulating you on winning a full scholarship to Space Camp. You will learn about space flight as you participate in the same kind of training that real astronauts complete. The letter asks you to write a paragraph either accepting or declining the offer. What would you say? Write the paragraph here.

_____

_____

_____

_____

_____

_____

Singular nouns name one person, place, thing, or idea.
Plural nouns name more than one.

Complete this paragraph using the plural forms of the missing words.

Peter looked around the _____ . There were _____ and
cage   kitten

_____ , _____ and _____ . There were even some
puppy   mouse   hamster

_____ . The SPCA had _____ for everyone. He walked up and
sheep   animal

down the _____ trying to make up his mind. The _____ watched
aisle   animal

him with bright _____ . Some voiced _____ , and some moved back
eye   greeting

into the _____ of their _____ . Peter wished that he could adopt
corner   cubicle

them all.

MATH TIME

Complete the input/output charts.

Input	8	10	12	
Output	2	4		8

Input	5	10	15	
Output	1	2	3	

Input	3	6	9	
Output	4	8	12	

Find the groups of words that are sentences. Add end punctuation and write the word sentence on the line following each complete sentence. Add words to each fragment to make it into a sentence. Write your new sentences on the lines at the bottom.

Climbed the rock and rested _____

The leaves rustled in the wind _____

The basketball swished through the net _____

Pete, Anna, and Paul _____

Did he go home _____

_____

_____

_____

MATH TIME

Find the answers.

1. Andy likes to ride his bike. He can ride from his house to school in 10 minutes, from school to Juan's house in 12 minutes, from Juan's house to the mall in 7 minutes, and from the mall to his house in 17 minutes. How long will it take Andy to ride from school to the mall, if he rides by Juan's house on the way? _____

2. Carla wants to see a movie with her friends to celebrate her birthday. The matinee costs $2.50 and the evening show costs $4.00. If her mother gives her $30.00 to pay for tickets, how many people (including Carla) can go to the matinee? To the evening show?

   _____ matinee

   _____ evening show

3. Marcos is 48 inches tall. His younger brother, Jose, is 9 inches shorter than Marcos. His older brother, Raul, is 16 inches taller than Jose. How tall is Raul?

   _____ inches

   _____ feet & inches

Friday

Week 3

Buried Treasure

Here are the directions for pacing the way to the buried treasure. Shade in the squares as you go.

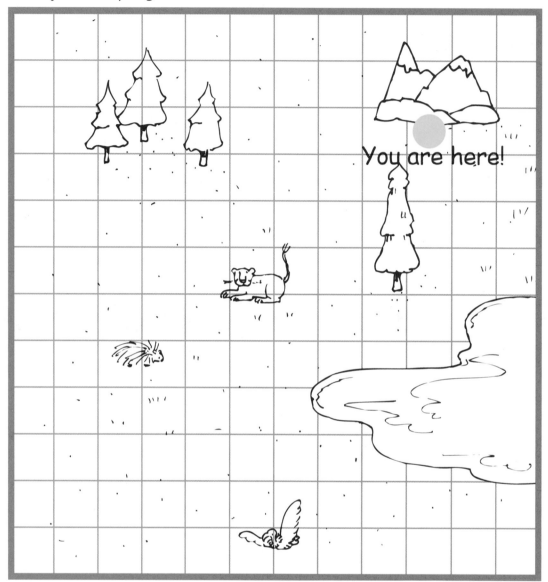

You are here!

1. Four paces south
2. Six paces west
3. Three paces north
4. Two paces west
5. Eight paces south

6. Five paces east
7. Seven paces north
8. One step east
9. Three paces north
10. Dig!

What do you think you will find?

_____

_____

Color a  for each page finished.

Parent's Initials

Monday ☆☆ _____

Tuesday ☆☆ _____

Wednesday ☆☆ _____

Thursday ☆☆ _____

Friday ☆☆ _____

Spelling Words

knot	neighbor
knight	whole
knowledge	limb
unknown	climb
gnat	written
gnaw	wrong

A Memorable Moment

What sticks in your mind about this week?
Write about it.

Keeping Track

Color a book for every 15 minutes you read.

Monday	Tuesday	Wednesday	Thursday	Friday

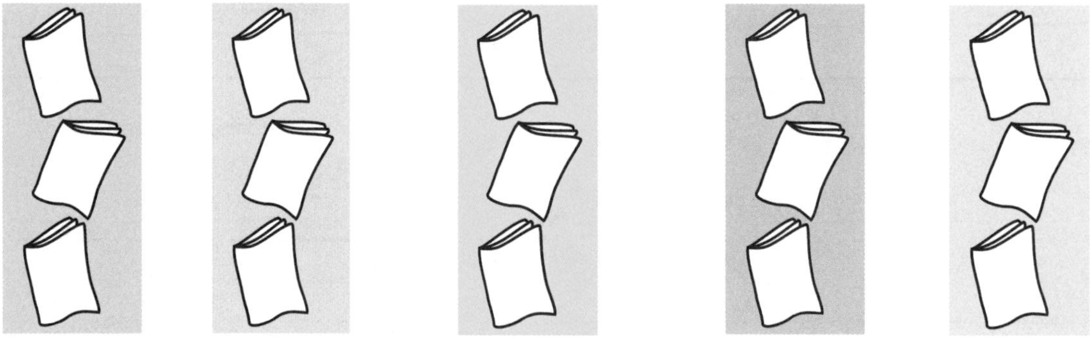

List four events from a book you are reading. Put them in the order they happened.

Allen Say was born in Yokohama, Japan. When he was six years old, he decided that he wanted to be a cartoonist. However, the world was at war. In the midst of the war, he attended seven different elementary schools. When the war ended, Allen was sent to live with his grandmother. He didn't get along with her, so he was allowed to live alone in a one-room apartment. He was twelve years old when he apprenticed himself to a famous Japanese cartoonist, Noro Shinpei.

He spent the next four years drawing and painting.

When Allen was sixteen, his father moved with Allen to the United States. Allen went to a military school in California for one year and then struck out on his own. He moved from job to job, city to city, and school to school. He painted his way through California before he opened a photography studio.

Today Allen Say is a successful writer, illustrator, and photographer. Many of his books tell about parts of his life. His autobiographical story, *Grandfather's Journey*, won the Caldecott Medal in 1993. He says that it is a joyous experience to tell a story with his brush.

1. What was Allen Say's ambition?

_____

2. What was unusual about young Allen's life?

_____

_____

3. What does it mean to "apprentice oneself to another person"?

_____

_____

4. What do you do that is a joyous experience?

_____

_____

Check in your public library for a book written by Allen Say. *The Apprentice's Ink* is a chapter book that tells about his time as an apprentice.

Monday

Week 4

1. prof mansour read a poem called family time and then he singed a song called we is family

_____

_____

2. mr williams how much does these flowers cost carmen asked

_____

_____

3. how many pancakes does you want the cook ask us

_____

_____

MATH TIME

Find the answers.

9)48 7)56 2)46 6)72 5)65 4)64 3)78 8)104

6)90 8)128 3)81 7)105 5)80 2)38 4)76 9)117

7)84 5)210 9)81 2)34 8)480 3)72 6)84 4)90

Spell It!

Cross out the silent letter(s) in each of the words below. Then use the words to complete the sentences.

knot   wrong   unknown   climbed   neighbor   whole   limb

1. My _____ rescued my kitten when it _____ out

   on the _____.

2. The letter came to the _____ address, so I wrote

   _____ on the envelope.

3. Sue's stomach was tied in a _____ as she got ready to give the speech.

Copy these sentences in your best handwriting.

Marvelous, magnificent Monday,
Totally terrific Tuesday,
Wild and wonderful Wednesday,
Thoroughly thrilling Thursday,
And finally, fun-filled Friday.
What a week!

_____

- -

_____

- -

_____

- -

_____

- -

_____

Tuesday

Week 4

Language Lines

Most plural nouns end in **s**, but some nouns have irregular plural forms or do not change at all.

Use the correct plural form for each singular noun in the sentences below.

1. All the _____ and _____ got into the lifeboats before the _____.
   woman   child   man

2. Be sure to wash your _____ and brush your _____ before you go to bed.
                          foot   tooth

3. The people saw flocks of _____, groups of _____, and herds
                              goose   moose

   of _____ in the forest.
      deer

MATH TIME

Write the numbers.

Write the following numbers in standard form.

two hundred eighty-nine   _____

one thousand five hundred thirty-five _____

seven hundred seventy-two   _____

ten thousand sixty-nine   _____

Write the following numbers in word form.

682   _____

897   _____

1,268 _____

12,043 _____

Week 4

Tuesday

Cut & Paste
a Story

When Lois Ehlert went to art school, she discovered that she liked cutting and pasting better than she liked drawing. It was hard to move the parts of a drawing around, but if shapes were cut out of paper they could be moved before they were glued down. So Ms. Ehlert focused on creating collages. She glued scraps of fabric, ribbon, wire, wrapping paper, plastic, cardboard, seeds, buttons, tree bark, and cardboard flaps. She formed the "found" materials into pictures of the animals, flowers, and trees she loved.

Today Lois Ehlert lives in Milwaukee, Wisconsin. She uses colorful collages to illustrate the children's books she writes. When she wrote *Eating the Alphabet,* she spent a year visiting her local grocery store, buying fruits and vegetables, creating bright, bold collages, and eating! Ms. Ehlert says that every book requires hard work, endless research, and a special idea for presenting the information to her readers.

1. Why did Ms. Ehlert like cutting and pasting better than drawing?

_____

_____

2. What is a collage?

_____

_____

3. What does "found" materials mean in this article?

_____

_____

4. Lois Ehlert says that everyone needs a special space for keeping all the things for creating. What things would you keep in your special space? What would you create with those things?

_____

_____

©2005 by Evan-Moor Corp. • Daily Summer Activities 4–5 • EMC 1031

Language Lines

The tense of a verb tells when an action occurs.

Underline the verbs in the paragraph below.
Write a P over the verb if it happened in the past.
Write PR over the verb if it happens in the present.
Write an F over the verb if it will happen in the future.

My cousin promised that she would come for the weekend. She called me last night to say she is coming this evening. She will arrive about 7:00 p.m. Mom is fixing her favorite dessert as a surprise. We will have a party while she is here.

MATH TIME

Find the coordinates.

What are the coordinates of x, y, and z on this graph?

x = _____

y = _____

z = _____

Mark a new point (6, 9). Name the point with the first initial of your name.

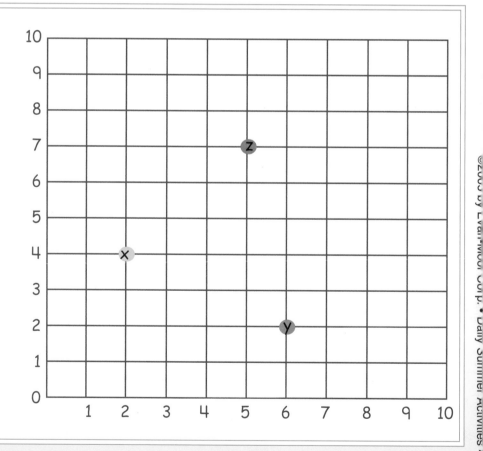

Week 4   Wednesday

Geography

Use a ruler and the map scale to measure the distance between these locations.

Brazil

From	To	Approximate Distance
Rio de Janeiro	Brasília	_____
São Paulo	Pôrto Alegre	_____
Pôrto Velho	Brasília	_____

Find two cities on the map that are about 400 km apart.

_____ _____

In My Own Words...

Make a new word. Use parts of existing words if you'd like. Write your word in the box.

What does your word mean? Write its definition.

_____

Use your word in a sentence.

_____

Write about what might happen if you used your new word in a conversation.

_____

_____

Language Lines

We add ed to many verbs to make the past tense. Other verbs have spelling changes. These are called irregular verbs.

Write the past tense for these verbs.

present	past	present	past
begin	_____	choose	_____
grow	_____	eat	_____
run	_____	know	_____
throw	_____	drink	_____
think	_____	write	_____
make	_____	swing	_____

MATH TIME

Can you put the numbers in order?

1. Rewrite these numbers in order from smallest to largest.

8.00	8.30	0.800	0.83
_____	_____	_____	_____
smallest			largest

57,327	5,703,275	573,275	5,732
_____	_____	_____	_____
smallest			largest

2. Write >, <, or = in the circles to make a true statement.

65.73 ◯ 65.81   2 ◯ 1.3   81.0 ◯ 81.00   3 x 4 ◯ 6 x 2

©2003 by Evan-Moor Corp. • Daily Summer Activities 4-5 • EMC 1031

Pronouns are used as substitutes for nouns.

Circle the pronouns in these sentences. Then write the nouns to which the pronouns refer.

1. Greg invited Andy to his birthday party. _____

2. Mario and Lee went to the aquarium because they wanted to see the new exhibit.

   _____

3. Elise said that she was too busy to do her homework last night. _____

4. Andrea was too big for her old bike, so she sold it at a garage sale. _____

5. The carpenter built the house and then sold it. _____

MATH TIME   Find the answers.

1. Kiko likes to fish. She caught an 8 pound 3 ounce trout at Ranger Lake. The record catch so far for the season is 129 ounces. Did Kiko's fish break the record? (16 ounces = 1 pound)   _____

2. Ian is playing a video game. If he started playing at 3:45 p.m. when he got home from school and stops playing at 6:15 p.m., how long will Ian have played?   _____

3. Sue and Penny have the same numerals in their addresses—1, 3, 5, 6, 7, 8, and 9. Sue's number is the smallest number that can be created with the seven numbers, and Penny's is the largest number. What are the girls' addresses?   _____

Friday   Week 4

Building Your Vocabulary

Word Box

- case
- hushed
- wish
- sienna
- skin
- sensitive
- droned
- day
- conversation
- witnessed
- sorrow
- dismay
- speaks
- listened
- address
- black
- broken
- special
- peels

Across

1. unusual, out of the ordinary
4. not whole, in pieces
6. to speak to
8. talks
9. great sadness
11. 24-hour period
12. easily affected by conditions
15. shade of brown
16. quiet, low in volume

Down

2. pulls back to remove
3. talk between people
4. opposite of white
5. paid attention in order to hear
7. frightened amazement
10. saw or observed in person
11. spoke in a dull, monotonous tone
12. outer covering
13. desire, hope
14. evidence or argument for

WEEK 5

Color a for each page finished.

Parent's Initials

Monday ☆ ☆ _____

Tuesday ☆ ☆ _____

Wednesday ☆ ☆ _____

Thursday ☆ ☆ _____

Friday ☆ ☆ _____

Spelling Words

believe	might
chief	height
niece	tried
deceive	describe
received	triangle
agree	variety

A Memorable Moment

What sticks in your mind about this week? Write about it.

_____

_____

_____

_____

Keeping Track

Color a book for every 15 minutes you read.

Monday	Tuesday	Wednesday	Thursday	Friday

Could the events in the book you are reading really happen? Explain.

_____

_____

_____

_____

Loy Krathong

Thailand make little boats from banana leaves. They decorate the sides of their krathongs with colorful flowers and place a candle inside each boat. At nighttime the children light the candles, make a wish, and watch as their krathongs float down the river. Legend says that if the candle stays lit until the krathong disappears, the wish will come true.

Loy Krathong is a special holiday celebrated in Thailand. Loy means "float" and krathong means "leaf cup." During the festival, the children of

1. What is Loy Krathong?

_____

_____

2. What would you do to celebrate Loy Krathong?

_____

_____

3. Write a wish you might make as you put your krathong in the river.

_____

4. There are other customs about doing a certain thing to make wishes come true. List several of these customs.

_____

_____

_____

_____

Monday

Week 5

1. the twins got to write thank-you notes for there birthday presents

_____

_____

2. how many books did you reed this summer asked miss gonzales

_____

_____

3. i just finished reading harriet the spy anita told henry

_____

_____

MATH⊙TIME

Find the answers.

584	467	738	197	625	393
+ 392	- 232	+ 295	- 126	+ 316	- 204

37	41	96	27	58	41
x 9	x 8	x 6	x 7	x 5	x 9

$$8\overline{)640} \qquad 7\overline{)497} \qquad 9\overline{)828} \qquad 6\overline{)564}$$

Spell It!

Circle the misspelled words in the sentences. Then write them correctly on the lines.

1. Do you beleive that Sammy will agre to help at the vareity show?

_____   _____   _____

2. I tryed to descripe the triangel for him.

_____   _____   _____

3. The cheef meite choose the ladder because of its highth.

_____   _____   _____

4. My kneece receeved the gift that I sent.

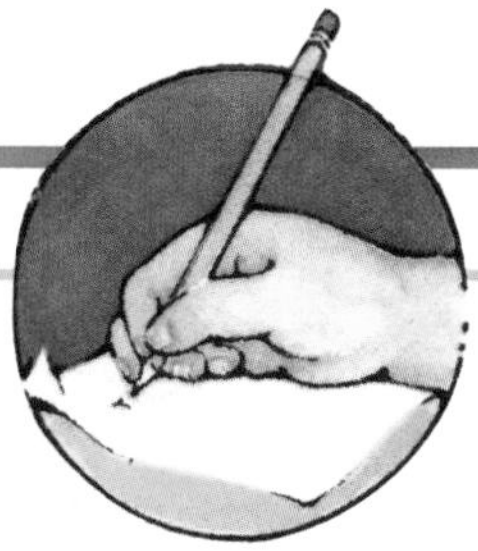

_____   _____

Handwriting

Pp

Copy these sentences.
Practice making your p's correctly.

Peacocks parade in purple plumes.

_____
_____
_____

Pink peony poses for a portrait.

_____
_____
_____

Underline the possessive words in these sentences.
Add apostrophes where they are needed to show ownership.

1. The suns rays melted the ice cream.
2. The students portfolios were stored in the file.
3. The dogs leashes broke as they chased the cat across the field.
4. The girls skateboard was left on the playground.

Write a sentence with a possessive that uses 's.

_____

_____

Write a sentence with a possessive that uses s'.

_____

_____

MATH TIME

Continue the patterns.

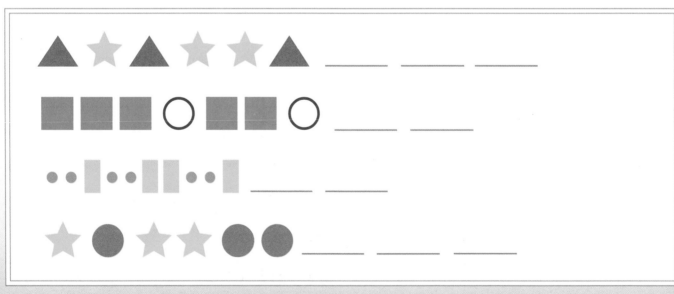

The Science Project

Just before the bell rang, Mr. Nielsen said, "Don't forget that your science projects are due a week from today."

Jose thought about his project. A few days ago, he had found frog eggs at the pond near his house. He had scooped up a dozen or so eggs and some pond water in an empty jar. At home, he placed the jar on top of the refrigerator to stay warm. The eggs looked like small black beads in white jelly.

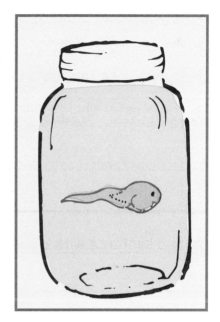

Each day, Jose looked at the eggs through a magnifying glass and drew what he saw. Day by day, he watched the jelly part of the eggs get smaller as the tadpoles grew in the black centers. Soon he could see heads and tails, and the tadpoles began to move. His science book said that the jelly part was food for the growing tadpoles.

The next Thursday, the first of the eggs hatched. A tiny tadpole stuck itself to a leaf of the pond plant Jose had put in the jar. It had no mouth yet, but Jose could see fingerlike gills behind its head.

By Friday, four more eggs had hatched. Jose carefully carried the jar to school, along with his day-by-day drawings and his journal of the changes he'd seen.

"This is a fine project, Jose," said Mr. Nielsen. "You must have given it a lot of thought."

Number these sentences in the order in which they happened.

_____ After six days the tadpoles began to hatch.

_____ On Friday, Jose took his science project to school.

_____ Mr. Nielsen liked Jose's science project.

_____ Jose found frog eggs in the pond and took some home in a jar.

_____ The young tadpoles had gills but no mouths.

_____ Each day the black part of the eggs grew to look more like tadpoles.

Some possessives do not need apostrophes.

Circle the possessive form in each of these sentences.

1. The dog wagged its tail.

2. We spent our summer at camp.

3. My hat is on the table.

4. The roosters held their heads high.

Write a sentence that uses a possessive that does <u>not</u> need an apostrophe.

_____

_____

MATH⏱TIME   Find the answers.

1. Rafael can run one mile in 8.5 minutes. If he
   keeps up this speed, how long will it take him
   to run 5 miles?   _____

2. Maria is selling T-shirts for her choir. Each
   shirt sells for $8. The choir keeps half of
   that as profit. If she sells 14 shirts, how
   much money will she have earned for the choir?   _____

3. Abby is half as old as her dad, but twice as old
   as her brother Sal. If Sal is 11, how old is
   their dad?   _____

Ge·graphy

Find what is located at these points.

Australia

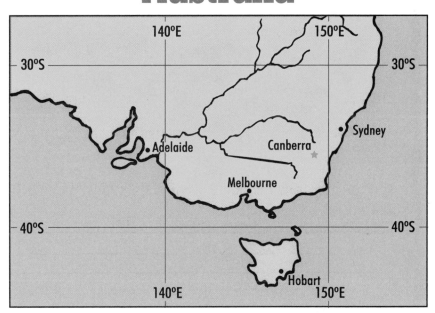

1. 35°S, 138°E

   _____

2. 36°S, 149°E

   _____

3. 43°S, 147°E

   _____

4. 38°S, 145°E

   _____

In My Own Words...

How Do You Play?

Write the directions for your favorite summer game.
- Start from the beginning.
- Make the directions easy to understand.
- Include a list of any special equipment needed.

_____

_____

_____

_____

_____

_____

_____

A comma is used to separate two or more adjectives listed together, unless one of the adjectives tells how many or is a color.

Add commas to the sentences below.

1. The little brown hen laid a round spotted egg.

2. Sami had bright curly ribbons in her long black hair.

3. Busy red ants scurried up the steep slippery sides of their hill.

4. Would you like three tall boys to help you carry the heavy bulging grocery bags?

Write a sentence about a girl and her dogs, using adjectives to describe how many and what kind.

_____

_____

MATH TIME

Draw a picture to go with each problem. Draw the wholes and shade the parts represented by the two fractions. Then write the answer.

$\frac{1}{2} + \frac{1}{2} =$ _____

$\frac{1}{4} + \frac{3}{4} =$ _____

$\frac{1}{3} + \frac{2}{3} =$ _____

$\frac{3}{4} + \frac{3}{4} =$ _____

$\frac{1}{6} + \frac{5}{6} =$ _____

$\frac{1}{8} + \frac{3}{8} =$ _____

Use this with singular nouns. Use these with plural nouns.

Complete each sentence using this or these.

1. _____ slice of cake is yummy.

2. Will you help me put _____ chairs away?

3. _____ is the steepest hill in the neighborhood.

4. I want to put _____ books in my backpack.

Write a sentence using this as an adjective.

_____

Write a sentence using these as an adjective.

_____

MATH TIME

The median is the middle.

Write the median of each set of numbers.

median

4, 7, 9, 10, 12, 14, 16 _____

1, 3, 5, 7, 9, 11, 13 _____

5, 10, 15, 20, 25 _____

30, 31, 32, 33, 34, 35, 36 _____

Syllogisms

Long ago in Greece, a famous thinker named Aristotle invented syllogisms. A syllogism has three sections. Facts are given in the first two sections. The third section is a new idea taken from the facts in the first two sections.

Example: All birds have feathers.
             Chickens are birds.
             Therefore, chickens have feathers.

A syllogism can be valid, without being true.

Example: All babies are cute.
             No cute things cry.
             Therefore, no babies cry.

Write the third line for each of the following syllogisms. Mark whether you think the syllogism is true or false.

All children like bubble gum.

All girls are children.

Therefore, _____.   True   False

All cats are purring animals.

All lions are cats.

Therefore, _____.   True   False

All stars are in the sky.

The sun is a star.

Therefore, _____.   True   False

All apples grow on trees.

Granny Smiths are apples.

Therefore, _____.   True   False

Week 5   Friday

Color a for each page finished.

Parent's Initials

Monday ☆ ☆ _____

Tuesday ☆ ☆ _____

Wednesday ☆ ☆ _____

Thursday ☆ ☆ _____

Friday ☆ ☆ _____

Spelling Words

without	something
myself	become
anybody	maybe
butterfly	outside
basketball	classroom
homework	secondhand

A Memorable Moment

What sticks in your mind about this week? Write about it.

_____

_____

_____

_____

_____

Keeping Track

Color a book for every 15 minutes you read.

Monday	Tuesday	Wednesday	Thursday	Friday

Describe a character that you read about this week.

_____

_____

_____

_____

The Peanut

The peanut is one of the most interesting plants in the world. Sometimes known as the "ground nut" or "goober pea," it has many uses. The peanut is a kind of pea. It is not a nut. It has seeds in pods like peas. However, while the pea plant's seedpods grow off its stem, the peanut grows its pods underground.

Peanuts are useful plants. Their seeds are tasty and healthy. Peanut oil is used to oil machinery and to make soap, face powder, shaving cream, shampoo, and paint. Peanut stems and leaves are used in livestock feed and to make fabrics. Even the shells are used to make plastics and wallboard.

The peanut plant is thought to have originated in Brazil or Peru. Portuguese explorers transported it to Africa. From Africa, the peanut was brought to America. Soldiers during the Civil War ate peanuts because they were inexpensive and high in protein. About 2.4 billion pounds of peanuts are consumed each year in the U.S.

1. What are two other names for peanuts?

_____   _____

2. Name some of the ways the different parts of a peanut plant are used.

seed _____

shell _____

stem and leaves _____

oil _____

3. How are peanuts different from other plants?

_____

_____

4. List several different ways that peanuts are eaten.

_____

_____

Monday

Week 6

(71)

1. to make the pizza crust mr toscano through the doe into the air

_____

_____

2. she called shannon her best friend to find out when the picnic will began

_____

_____

3. watch out there is broken glass on the floor yelled peter

_____

_____

MATH TIME Find the answers.

19	18	33	16	345	19	25
26	37	22	18	80	20	11
+ 23	+ 28	+ 36	+ 25	+ 349	+ 9	+ 27

29	17	17	38	62	39	17
35	13	6	19	166	19	15
+ 18	+ 15	+ 7	+ 37	+ 141	+ 27	+ 28

Spell It!

Write the two words that make up each of these compound words. Draw a line to divide each word into syllables. Then write the number of syllables in each compound word.

without   _____   _____   _____

myself   _____   _____   _____

anybody   _____   _____   _____

butterfly   _____   _____   _____

basketball   _____   _____   _____

homework   _____   _____   _____

something   _____   _____   _____

secondhand   _____   _____   _____

Handwriting

Copy these lines from the famous poem "Sea Fever" by John Masefield. Use your best handwriting.

I must go down to the seas again, to the lonely sea and the sky, And all I ask is a tall ship and a star to steer her by.

_____

_____

_____

_____

_____

©2005 by Evan-Moor Corp. • Daily Summer Activities 4-5 • EMC 1031

Use er to compare two nouns. Use est to compare three or more nouns.

Add er or est to each of the adjectives to complete the sentences.

1. Lizzie is the fast_____ runner in the class.

2. Tyrone is tall_____ than Syd.

3. The fire alarm is the loud_____ thing I've ever heard.

4. A bratwurst is fatt_____ than a hot dog.

Write a sentence comparing two things.

_____

Write a sentence comparing three or more things.

_____

MATH TIME

How many containers will you need if...?

4 fish fit in a can	11 fish fit in a box	18 fish fit in a crate

number of fish	cans	boxes	crates
16	4	2	1
9			
25			
37			
45			
75			

©2003 by Evan-Moor Corp. • Daily Summer Activities 4–5 • EMC 1031

George Washington Carver
1864-1943

George Washington Carver grew up as a slave on a plantation in Missouri. As a boy, George loved plants! By the time he was seven, people in Diamond Grove, Missouri, called him "The Plant Doctor."

George was a skinny child with a high voice. He stuttered when he talked, but he was determined to learn as much as he could. When he was ten, he left home to find a town that would allow black children to go to school. He traveled through Missouri and Kansas, going to schools that would accept black students, until he graduated from high school. He opened his own laundry to pay his expenses.

In 1890, George began college. He studied art and then agriculture. He was the first black graduate of Iowa State College. Thomas Edison asked George to come to work in his laboratory, but George turned him down. George said that he wanted to help his people. So he set up an agricultural department at Tuskegee Normal School, a new university for black students in Alabama.

George Washington Carver became known as the "Wizard of Tuskegee." His work was instrumental in improving farming in the South. He is especially remembered for his peanut research. He discovered how to make 300 different things from the peanut plant.

1. What words would you use to describe George Washington Carver?

___hard working___

_____

2. What makes Dr. Carver's story so inspirational?

___as he was ___

_____

___a good man.___

3. In this word search, find some of the products that Dr. Carver made from peanuts.

a	c	s	h	a	m	p	o	o	b	l
s	h	o	e	p	o	l	i	s	h	i
a	o	d	f	h	u	k	n	g	e	n
l	r	u	b	b	e	r	k	m	l	o
a	m	i	p	l	a	s	t	i	c	l
d	y	e	p	e	o	q	s	l	n	e
t	u	s	o	a	p	u	w	k	v	u
x	a	z	i	c	e	c	r	e	a	m
c	e	b	d	h	c	o	f	f	e	e
a	x	l	e	g	r	e	a	s	e	y

Word Box

salad	shoe polish	linoleum	dye
coffee	axle grease	soap	rubber
milk	plastic	shampoo	
bleach	ice cream	ink	

Language Lines

Homophones are words that sound the same but have different meanings.

Fill in the blanks in each pair of sentences using a pair of homophones from the box.

flower
flour
herd
heard
choose
chews
weak
week

1. Mallory _____ the baby crying.

   The _____ of cattle wandered across the fields.

2. I use whole wheat _____ when I make bread.

   She wore a yellow _____ in her hair.

3. Alonzo _____ the gum and then blows a bubble.

   Maria will _____ which frosting to put on the cake.

4. Use the remaining pair of homophones in a sentence.

   _____

MATH TIME

Find the answers.

1. In the number 26,195, what digit is in

   the thousands place?   _____

   the tens place?   _____

   the ten-thousands place?   _____

   the hundreds place?   _____

2. In the number 935,701, what digit is in

   the ones place?   _____

   the ten-thousands place?   _____

   the tens place?   _____

   the hundreds place?   _____

3. In the number 6,871,204, what digit is in

   the hundreds place?   _____

   the hundred-thousands place?   _____

   the millions place?   _____

   the ten-thousands place?   _____

4. In the number 1,067.4, what digit is in

   the tens place?   _____

   the tenths place?   _____

   the thousands place?   _____

   the ones place?   _____

Wednesday

Geography
Australia

This graph shows the population of the states and territories of Australia. Use the information to fill in the blanks and answer the question.

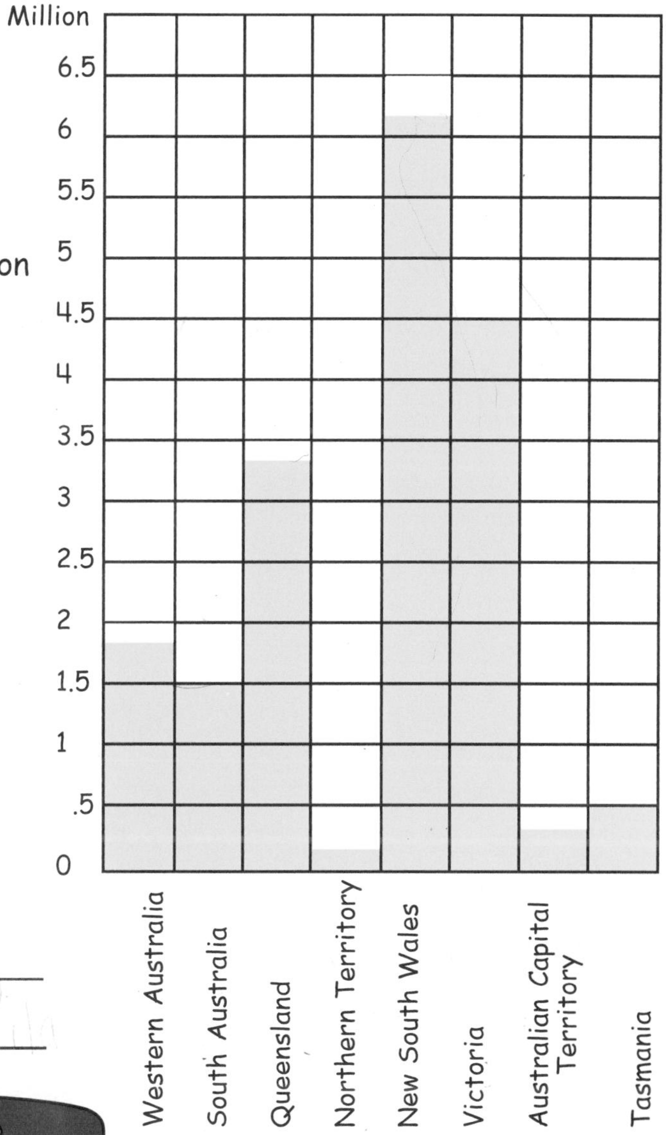

Western Australia _____

South Australia _____

Queensland _____

Northern Territory _____

New South Wales _____

Victoria _____

Australian Capital Territory _____

Tasmania _____

How does the population of Victoria compare with the population of South Australia?

_____

_____

Million

Graph y-axis labels (top to bottom): 6.5, 6, 5.5, 5, 4.5, 4, 3.5, 3, 2.5, 2, 1.5, 1, .5, 0

Graph x-axis labels: Western Australia, South Australia, Queensland, Northern Territory, New South Wales, Victoria, Australian Capital Territory, Tasmania

In My Own Words...

Summer Is Here!

Write a chant or a cheer for summer. Practice reading it aloud. You may even want to make up actions to go with your words.

Example:

Sunny day, sunny day,
Bright, bold, squinty ray,
Sunny day, sunny day,
Let's go out and play.

_____

_____

_____

_____

_____

Language Lines

Fill in the missing words.

1. The river ran _____ the bridge.

2. Did you get a letter _____ your grandma?

3. Maria went swimming _____ her friends.

4. I can take messages _____ Dad when he's not home.

5. Don't forget to put a stamp _____ the envelope.

6. Scott ate the largest piece _____ pizza.

Word Box	of under for from on with

Write a sentence using two of the words in the word box.

_____

_____

MATH⊙TIME

Find the answers.

1. Lanie and Fred are each collecting baseball cards. If Lanie has three times as many cards as Fred and she has 84, how many cards does Fred have?

_____

2. Terry has just set up a 10-gallon fish tank in his bedroom. He has 10 neon tetras, twice as many guppies as tetras, and half as many blue gouramis as tetras. How many fish does he have in all?

_____

3. Matt has 4 pet rats. Eric has 2 parakeets. Kirstin has 3 gerbils. If each pet eats one-quarter cup of food each day, how much food do they need altogether for 8 days?

_____

Write contractions to complete the sentences.

_____ going to the park to play. My friend Thomas _____ come with me.
 I am   can not

His mother _____ feeling well, so he will stay home. After _____ finished
                    is not   I have

playing, _____ go to the library and check out a book. Then _____ take the
              I will   I will

book over to Thomas so he _____ feel lonely.
                                    will not

MATH TIME

Solve the problems. Then use the key to answer the riddles.

What has eyes but cannot see? ____ ____ ____ ____ ____ ____

662	504	734	426	845	615
- 275	- 166	- 157	- 379	- 268	- 277

What has ears but cannot hear? ____ ____ ____ ____

356	723	783	912
- 278	- 385	- 388	- 667

What has a tongue but cannot talk? ____ ____ ____ ____

614	524	836	347
- 187	- 297	- 498	- 168

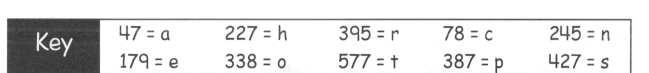

Key	47 = a	227 = h	395 = r	78 = c	245 = n
	179 = e	338 = o	577 = t	387 = p	427 = s

Read this recipe for making peanut butter candy.
Follow the directions and ask an adult to help.

MMMmmm. . .

Candy Marbles!!

What You Need

- ½ cup of chunky peanut butter
- ¼ cup of evaporated milk
- ¼ cup of brown sugar
- 1 teaspoon of cinnamon
- 1 cup of crispy chow mein noodles, slightly crushed
- 1 cup of stick pretzels, slightly crushed
- ½ cup of chopped nuts

What You Do

1. Stir the peanut butter, evaporated milk, brown sugar, and cinnamon together in a saucepan.
2. Cook over medium heat for five minutes.
3. Remove from heat. Stir in noodles, pretzels, and nuts.
4. Drop spoonfuls onto a foil-lined cookie sheet.
5. Chill for one hour.
6. Pop one in your mouth for a yummy treat!

Color a for each page finished.

Parent's Initials

Monday ⭐⭐ _____

Tuesday ⭐⭐ _____

Wednesday ⭐⭐ _____

Thursday ⭐⭐ _____

Friday ⭐⭐ _____

Spelling Words

photograph	often
alphabet	bought
nephew	thoughtless
enough	whose
cough	clue
half	refuse

A Memorable Moment

What sticks in your mind about this week? Write about it.

_____

_____

_____

_____

_____

Keeping Track

Color a book for every 15 minutes you read.

Monday	Tuesday	Wednesday	Thursday	Friday

Describe the setting of a story you read this week.

_____

_____

_____

_____

Jackie Robinson
Breaking the Color Barrier

Sometimes a tremendous change can occur through an individual's determination. Jackie Robinson overcame discrimination and segregation to change professional sports forever.

Jackie was a gifted athlete. Jackie was given a scholarship to UCLA. He participated in football, basketball, baseball, and track. He was the first four-sport athlete in the school's history. Despite his success in college, he couldn't play major league professional sports. Sports, like many other areas of American life at that time, were segregated. That meant that black players and white players did not play on the same team or against each other.

In 1945, a man named Branch Rickey was the general manager of the Brooklyn Dodgers baseball team. He thought it was time for black men to play in the major leagues. With the support of the baseball commissioner, Mr. Rickey asked Jackie Robinson to become a part of his team. He chose Jackie not only for his playing ability, but also for his strong character. Jackie signed a contract in 1945 to play for the Dodgers.

Jackie Robinson excelled in the game. He helped the Dodgers win several pennants and a World Series. He also earned a place in the Baseball Hall of Fame. Jackie Robinson was more than a sports hero, he paved the way in major league sports for other black athletes.

1. What four sports did Jackie participate in during his college career?

   _____   _____   _____   _____

2. The main idea of the story is:
   a. Jackie Robinson was a gifted athlete.
   b. Branch Rickey wanted black men to play in the major leagues.
   c. Jackie Robinson helped to desegregate professional sports.

3. Which words describe Jackie Robinson?

   brave   angry   determined   timid   talented

4. What does segregated mean?

   _____

Monday

Week 7

83

1. yes maurice I want you to correct the mistakes on this paper said mr yamaguchi

_____

_____

2. the clouds rolled in the sky turned dark and it began to snow

_____

_____

3. cody have drew a diagram of the heart lungs and liver of a mouse

_____

_____

MATH TIME

Find the mistakes and correct them.

```
     24              27              14              16
  4)96            2)54            7)91            5)85
    8               4               7               5
   16              14              21              35
   16               7              21              35
```

```
     12              21              13              14
  6)72            4)84            7)91            4)64
    6               8               7               4
   12               4              21              24
   12               4              21              24
```

Spell It!

Circle the letters in these spelling words that make an f sound.

photograph   nephew   cough

alphabet   enough   half

Choose words from the list above to complete the sentences.

1. Uncle Ted has a _____ of me in his wallet. When he says, "That's my

_____!" it makes me feel good.

2. The letter z is not in the first _____ of the _____.

Handwriting

Write the names of the months.
Use your best handwriting.

Jumpin' *January*   Marvelous *May*   Spirited *September*
Flag-waving *February*   Jazzy *June*   Orderly *October*
Mixed-up *March*   Jolly *July*   Next-to-last *November*
Alarming *April*   Ambitious *August*   Dazzling *December*

Language Lines

Write the correct abbreviation for each word.

Avenue _____   Street _____

Mister _____   tablespoon _____

foot _____   Junior _____

pound _____   quart _____

Doctor _____   centimeter _____

qt.	Ave.	lb.	Jr.	St.
tbsp.	cm	Mr.	Dr.	ft.

MATH TIME

Find the answers.

1. Maurice is three times as tall as his brother. If Maurice is 5 feet, 3 inches tall, how tall is his brother? (Hint: Change Maurice's height to inches.)

   _____

2. Betty has 15 beanbag animals. If she gives $\frac{1}{3}$ of them to her sister, how many will she have left?

   _____

3. Murphy is walking dogs to earn some spending money. If he gets paid $2.50 per dog and he needs $18.00, how many dogs must he walk?

   _____

The Arctic Tundra

The Arctic plains, called the tundra, are found in northern Canada and in the state of Alaska. The tundra is an example of a cold desert. It receives very little precipitation. The winters are long and harsh with very low temperatures, and the summers are short.

The Arctic tundra has a layer of permanently frozen subsoil three feet (about one meter) under the surface. Even in the summer, this layer does not thaw. When the surface snow and ice melt, the water cannot drain through the layer of permafrost. It stays on the surface of the tundra in bogs and ponds.

The region is cold and windy even in the summer. In spite of this, there are plants that grow on the tundra. Mosses and lichens are the most common plants, but there are also many varieties of flowering plants that bloom during the brief growing season.

1. What is the tundra?

_____

2. Describe its usual weather conditions.

_____

_____

3. Why do bogs and pools form on the surface of the tundra during the summer?

_____

_____

4. Name the most common plants growing on the tundra.

_____

5. How is the tundra different from the area where you live?

_____

_____

_____

Add commas to these sentences.

1. Tanya welcome to our class!

2. I can tell Jamal that you've been practicing.

3. I can help you Monday Grandma.

4. Okay Mom. I'm on my way.

5. Sal can you tell me how to do this problem?

6. Hurry up Mark or we're going to be late.

MATH TIME

What is the perimeter of each shape?

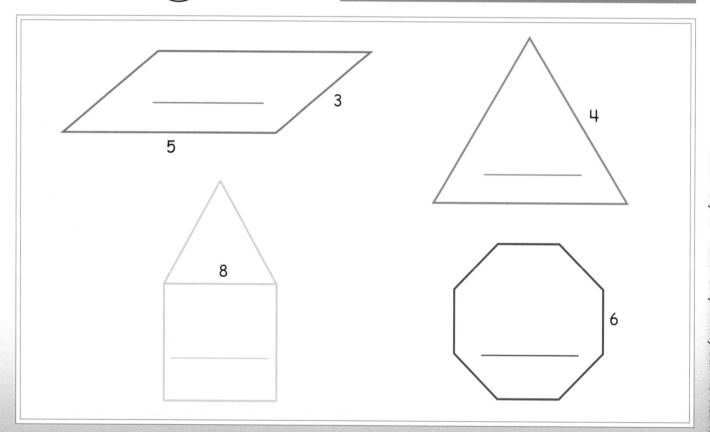

Week 7

Wednesday

Ge★graphy

Name the countries and the bodies of water marked on this map.

A. _____

B. _____

C. _____

D. _____

E. _____

F. _____

G. _____

H. _____

United States, Canada, Mexico, Atlantic Ocean, Pacific Ocean, Gulf of Mexico, Hudson Bay, Bering Sea

In My Own Words...

That's Alliteration!

Write three sentences in which every word begins with the same sound. **Begin by trying** one with your own name.　　　Jill jumped John's juniper joyfully.

1. _____

　 _____

2. _____

　 _____

3. _____

　 _____

Add commas to this letter.

410 Park Street
Funville Ohio
July 30 2000

Dear Pete

    Thank you for the super new shirt. I like the logo the color and the material. You sure know how to pick out a good present! I hope that you can come to visit soon. We can go to the zoo have a picnic and see a movie. Thanks again.

Your pal
Fred

MATH TIME

Find the answers.

2,317	4,139	5,216	5,349	3,725	3,148
+ 1,425	- 2,524	+ 1,208	- 2,616	+ 5,215	- 2,607

3,522	6,417	7,346	1,509	5,537	2,424
+ 4,138	- 2,514	+ 2,129	- 1,274	+ 4,127	- 1,028

Week 7

Thursday

Add quotation marks to these sentences.

1. How long will the movie last? wondered Tamara.

2. Fernando, will you get the bat? asked Coach Danley.

3. On the way home from the pool, Simon said, I can't wait to warm up!

4. I can't eat spinach, said Fred. I might turn green!

MATH TIME

What time is it?

_____   _____   _____

_____   _____   _____

Friday   Week 7

Number Puzzles

1. Choose 3 different digits from one to nine.

2. Make the largest and the smallest numbers you can from the three digits.

3. Subtract the smaller number from the larger number.

4. Reverse the order of the digits in the answer and add it to the original answer.

5. Write down the answer.

$$3, 2, 1$$

$$
\begin{array}{r}
3\,2\,1 \\
-\,1\,2\,3 \\
\hline
1\,9\,8 \\
+\,8\,9\,1 \\
\hline
1{,}0\,8\,9
\end{array}
$$

Try it with 3 more different digits.	Try it with 4 different digits.

How did the answer change from 3 digits to 4 digits?

_____

Do you think the same thing will happen
if you try it with 5 digits?   Yes   No

Try it and see.

Color a  for each page finished.

Parent's Initials

Monday ☆ ☆ _____

Tuesday ☆ ☆ _____

Wednesday ☆ ☆ _____

Thursday ☆ ☆ _____

Friday ☆ ☆ _____

Spelling Words

truth	voice
due	noise
menu	disappoint
future	voyage
used	loyal
news	destroy

A Memorable Moment

What sticks in your mind about this week? Write about it.

_____

_____

_____

_____

Keeping Track

Color a book for every 15 minutes you read.

Monday	Tuesday	Wednesday	Thursday	Friday

Think about the books you read this week. Tell about a character's problem and how it was solved.

_____

_____

_____

_____

Ordering from a Catalog

Fill in the order form below as if you were ordering the three items shown.
Pretend that your shoe size is 8 and that you want a silver helmet.

Safe Landing Protective Pack

#L69398

One size, adjustable
5-piece set. Knee, elbow, and
wrist pads. Foam inner lining
with hard plastic outside covers
for the knees and elbows.

Weight: 2.2 lbs.

Price: $18.69

Dial-a-Size Helmet

#M89356

Adjustable, fits most
adults. Red, blue, or silver. Safety
helmets suitable for most sports
except motorcycling. Air vents.

Weight: 2.8 lbs.

Price: $41.20

Lightning In-line Skates

#C97321

One-piece construction.
Vented polyurethane boot with
comfort insoles. Y class bearings and
medium-hard wheels. Long-lasting,
with a feel for the road. Rink safe.

Adult sizes 6, 7, 8, 9, 10, 11, 12

Weight: 8 lbs.

Price: $51.98

Order Now!

ORDER FORM

| Name: First | Middle Initial | Last | | Area Code | Telephone | |

| Address | | City | | State | Zip Code | |

Item	Catalog Number	Weight	Size	Color	Price

Shipping and Handling Charges

Weight	Delivery Charges
0–4.9 lbs.	$6.00
5–9.9 lbs.	$8.00
10–19.9 lbs.	$12.50
20–34.9 lbs	$15.00

For each additional pound over 34.9 add 25¢. Total the weight for the entire order before adding the shipping and handling charges.

Total price of order: _____

Total weight: _____

Shipping & handling: _____

Amount owed: _____

1. sean had ate popcorn nachos and too hot dogs at the ball game

_____

_____

2. him and me got a reward for finding jeannies lost dog

_____

3. your parents is celebrating there fifteenth anniversary in august

_____

_____

 **Find the answers.**

1. The sleepover party ended at 11:30 a.m. If the party lasted 16 hours and 30 minutes, at what time did the party start? _____

2. Sven can buy a candy bar from the grocery store for 30 cents, but the gas station sells them three for $1.00. Which is the better buy? _____

3. Diego was traveling about 30 miles per hour while racing his dirt bike. If he kept up this speed for one and one-half hours, about how many miles would he have traveled? _____

Spell It!

Fill in the missing letters.

oi	oy

v____ce   l____al

v____age   disapp____nt

n____se   destr____

u	ew	ue

tr____th   n____s

d____   ____sed

men____   f____ture

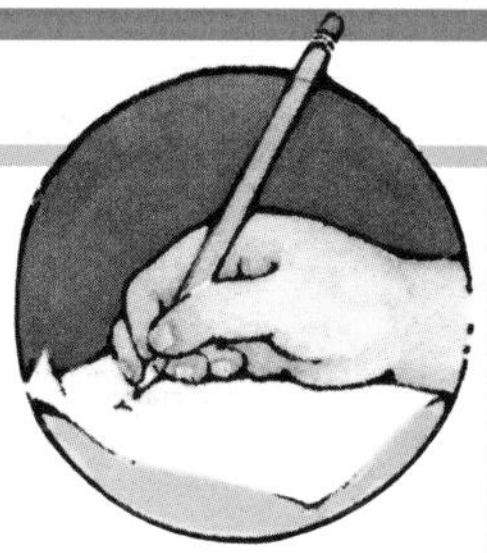

Write these ice-cream flavors.

Handwriting

rocky road and vanilla
strawberry and bubble gum
butter pecan and chocolate
cookies 'n cream and lemon sour

_____
_____
_____
_____
_____
_____

What's your favorite flavor? Why?
_____
_____

Copy these sentences. Use capital letters where they are needed.

1. my friend joyce lives in evanston illinois.

_____

_____

2. dr cook said that i could get my cast off on august 4.

_____

_____

3. jo said that jungle book was her favorite movie.

_____

_____

MATH TIME

Find the answers.

51	67	38	24	45	26	75	96
x 65	x 54	x 72	x 93	x 36	x 58	x 92	x 29

74	93	48	13	71	86	59	27
x 86	x 24	x 75	x 83	x 20	x 46	x 38	x 69

Colorful Ramblings from a **Crayon Box**

"Boy, is it crowded in here! That Jungle Green is in my spot! Will you please move? I wish they would make these boxes bigger!"

"Stop complaining! Soon one of us will be lost or broken, and then there'll be plenty of room."

I listened and observed as the hushed conversation in my crayon box droned on. It was a new 64-color box with a tight lid and bright yellow and green triangles covering its front.

Few crayon users realize that crayons not only speak, but they also have feelings. Just the other day, I witnessed the dismay of a Canary Yellow whose tip was nibbled off by a hungry artist. Have you ever seen the sorrow of a 20-color box that lost its black? Imagine life without a black! You see, crayons have the sensitive souls of artists.

The next time you use a crayon, think about the fragile feelings hidden under the ripped paper covering. Think of the shame and hopelessness in the lost-crayon tub. Take the time to return your crayons to their rightful home. Use them wisely so that their creative potential is realized.

1. From whose point of view is this story being told?

_____

2. What do you think is the purpose of this story?
   a. to give directions
   b. to inform
   c. to entertain

3. There is a recommendation for crayon users in the story. What is it?

_____

_____

_____

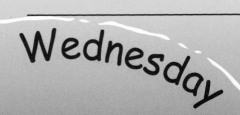

Week 8

Use I or me in each sentence.

1. _____ am learning to cook.

2. Aunt Carol wants _____ to weed her garden.

3. Maybe she will let _____ pick some carrots and squash.

4. Mom and _____ could make soup.

Write a sentence using I correctly.

_____

Write a sentence using me correctly.

_____

MATH TIME

Name each shape. Count the sides and corners. Then write a description of each shape.

Name _____ sides _____ corners _____

_____

_____

Name _____ sides _____ corners _____

_____

_____

Name _____ sides _____ corners _____

_____

_____

Geography

Locate each body of water on this map. Write its letter.

_____ Caribbean Sea

_____ Gulf of California

_____ Arctic Ocean

_____ Great Lakes

_____ Rio Grande

_____ Mississippi River

Color the land green.

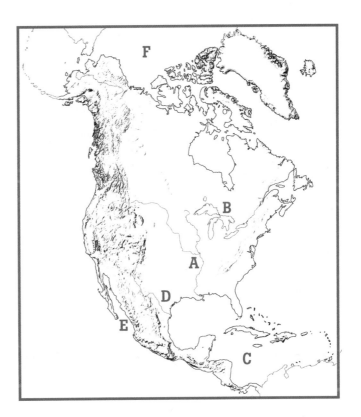

In My Own Words...

What Animal Are You Like?

Compare yourself to an animal. Tell how you are like that animal and in what ways you are different.

_____

_____

_____

_____

_____

_____

_____

Language Lines

Circle the correct words.

1. How _____ did you do?

2. _____ kittens are growing bigger.

3. _____ that boy standing by the pool?

4. Cookies fresh out of the oven taste so _____.

5. Do you know _____ hat this is?

6. When _____ you going on vacation?

good	well
Are	Our
Who's	Whose
good	well
who's	whose
are	our

MATH TIME

Find the answers.

Solve the problems, if $\triangledown$ equals 4.

$\triangledown + 8 = $ ____ $\triangledown - 3 = $ ____ $\triangledown \times 9 = $ ____ $\triangledown\overline{)88}$

$\triangledown + 12 = $ ____ $51 - 9\triangledown = $ ____ $\triangledown\triangledown0 + 3\triangledown = $ ____ $\triangledown\overline{)\triangledown\triangledown\triangledown\triangledown}$

Solve the problems, if $\triangledown$ equals 8.

$\triangledown + 8 = $ ____ $\triangledown - 3 = $ ____ $\triangledown \times 9 = $ ____ $\triangledown\overline{)88}$

$\triangledown + 12 = $ ____ $9\triangledown - 51 = $ ____ $\triangledown\triangledown0 + 3\triangledown = $ ____ $\triangledown\overline{)\triangledown\triangledown\triangledown\triangledown}$

Circle all the nouns in this list.

bake	school	long	Tom
truck	Mr. Gorze	wash	park
Trina	hospital	friend	pickle
feather	watermelon	Disneyland	purple

Write the nouns you circled in the correct category.

Person	Place	Thing
_____	_____	_____
_____	_____	_____
_____	_____	_____
_____	_____	_____

Help fill in the chart.

Maria is setting up a lemonade stand. She will sell a glass of lemonade for 20 cents and a cookie for 25 cents. Help her complete the chart she will use.

	Cost of Lemonade	Cost of Cookies	Cost of Lemonade + Cookies
1	20 cents	25 cents	45 cents
2			
3			
4			
5			
6			

Friday   Week 8

What Is It?

(16, 20)	(16, 3)	(12, 2)	(24, 20)	(8, 21)	(23, 2)	(7, 4)
(21, 12)	(23, 23)	(21, 10)	(19, 5)	(17, 19)	(20, 7)	(22, 8)
(22, 1)	(4, 14)	(24, 21)	(3, 7)	(23, 18)	(18, 18)	(18, 20)
(3, 9)	(22, 17)	(16, 1)	(14, 1)	(16, 6)	(6, 19)	(24, 19)
(8, 6)	(23, 5)	(20, 3)	(7, 3)	(3, 5)	(23, 22)	(14, 21)
(15, 1)	(5, 2)	(10, 22)	(12, 4)	(12, 3)	(24, 3)	(3, 12)
(7, 2)	(10, 5)	(12, 22)	(24, 5)	(17, 2)	(6, 2)	(21, 14)
(21, 8)	(3, 3)	(8, 7)	(13, 1)	(16, 4)	(21, 16)	(5, 17)

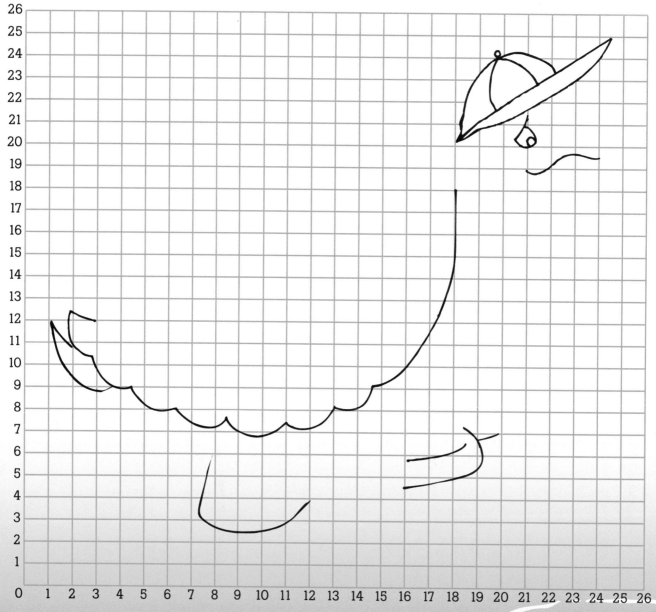

Week 8

Friday

©2005 by Evan-Moor Corp. • Daily Summer Activities 4–5 • EMC 1031

Color a for each page finished.

Parent's Initials

Monday ☆ ☆ _____

Tuesday ☆ ☆ _____

Wednesday ☆ ☆ _____

Thursday ☆ ☆ _____

Friday ☆ ☆ _____

Spelling Words

although	minute
together	quarter
country	several
among	sure
cousin	trouble
favorite	which

A Memorable Moment

What sticks in your mind about this week? Write about it.

_____

_____

_____

_____

_____

Keeping Track

Color a book for every 15 minutes you read.

Monday	Tuesday	Wednesday	Thursday	Friday

List four events from a book you are reading. Put them in the order they happened.

_____

_____

_____

_____

©2000 by Evan-Moor Corp. • Daily Summer Activities 4–5 • EMC 1031

On Becoming a Climber

Have you ever tried rock climbing? Mountain goats seem to climb cliffs with ease. Their hooves rest on narrow ledges, and they spring across gaps with surety. They have no ropes to break potential falls and no chalk for sweaty palms. Faced with a similar rock cliff, the human climber often struggles upward. Secured by a harness and ropes, the two-footed, two-handed climber works hard to find a safe way to experience the excitement of reaching the top. Imagine yourself a part of such an adventure.

It is early morning. The sun casts a warm glow on the granite slab. The summit beckons. Ready for the challenge, you slip on your climbing shoes, buckle your harness, and prepare for the ascent.

As you push yourself against the steep face, a chill fills your body. The rock has a long vertical crack. Automatically your hands chalk up. You take a deep breath and jam one hand into the narrow crack, twist it, and inch upward. You continue to jam a foot, then a hand, and reach upward at the same time. Sweat coats your face and drips down your back. You haul yourself up, hook into the anchor, and signal your belayer below, "Off belay!"

Congratulations on your climb! You have experienced the success of ascent. You share this exhilaration with the nimble-footed mountain goat.

1. What are three characteristics that would help a person be a good rock climber?

_____ _____ _____

2. Why does the author compare the climber with a mountain goat?

_____

_____

3. What is the author's opinion of rock climbing?
   a. It is a tense, yet exhilarating sport.
   b. It is a sport for only a few.
   c. It is a really dangerous sport.

4. When the author says "a chill fills your body," it means
   a. the sun hasn't come out yet
   b. the climber is filled with anticipation of a difficult climb
   c. the climber is sick

Monday

Week 9

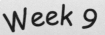107

1. my mom uses buttermilk to maek the doe

_____

_____

2. he phoned mike his partner to tell him about the match

_____

_____

3. hit the ball over the fence yelled steve

_____

_____

MATH TIME

Tell how much for one.

Show your work here.

3 for 99 cents   _____

$6 per dozen   _____

2 for $1.36   _____

$14.00 for 8   _____

24 for $1.44   _____

$8 for 32   _____

99 cents for 11   _____

Circle the words that are spelled correctly.

1. althoa	althoue	although
2. cousin	cusin	coesin
3. shure	sure	sher
4. whitch	wich	which
5. minet	minute	minit
6. truble	trahble	trouble

Copy this paragraph about owls.

Handwriting

Owls are nocturnal hunters.
They catch and eat small rodents.
In fact, a single barn owl can eat over
one thousand mice in just one year.

Add the missing punctuation marks.

comma ,	colon :	period .

1. Boston Massachusetts   4. Dallas Texas

2. March 7 1980   5. $23 95

3. 4 04 pm   6. July 4 1776

• Write today's date. _____

• Write the time._____

• Write the name of your city or town and state.

_____

MATH TIME   Find the answers.

1. Hallie is putting bowls in the cupboard. She can put a maximum of 4 bowls in each stack. If she has 18 bowls to put away, what is the minimum number of stacks Hallie will have?   _____

2. Mario is going to an amusement park. The park charges 50 cents per ride. Mario wants to ride all 19 rides at least once. What is the minimum amount of money he will need?   _____

3. John's kittens are playing outside. There are three more kittens in the barn than in the garden. There are two fewer kittens on the lawn than in the garden. If there are two kittens on the lawn, how many kittens does John have in all?   _____

One cold winter day, a boy went hunting. After he had shot several partridges, he sat down beside a great rock to rest. A deep voice came from the rock. "Listen, I will tell you a story." The boy jumped to his feet. There was no one around.

He called out, "Who are you? What is a story?"

"I am the Great Stone. I have been here since the beginning of time. I can tell you how things came to be," the voice rumbled from the rock.

The boy trembled at the power of the voice. Could it be the stone talking to him? He stood his ground and said, "Great Stone, tell your story."

"First, you must give me something," said the stone.

The boy took one of the partridges he had just killed and placed it on the rock. "Here is a bird for you, Great One. Now tell your story," said the boy, sitting back down.

The Great Stone began to speak. His words rumbled from the ground, telling a wonderful story of how the Earth had been made. As the stone spoke, the boy listened. He didn't feel the cold wind or snow. He seemed warm inside. When the story was over, the boy stood to leave. "Thank you, Great One. I must go share your story with my family. I will be back tomorrow."

1. What startled the boy at the beginning of the story?

_____

2. What exchange did the boy and the Great Stone make?

_____

_____

3. Did the boy like the story? Tell why you think the way you do.

_____

_____

4. A partridge is
   a. a type of bird
   b. a small rabbit
   c. a wild deer

5. Rumbled means
   a. laughed cheerfully
   b. spoke in soft, quiet tones
   c. made a deep, rolling sound

Language Lines

Use we or us in each sentence.

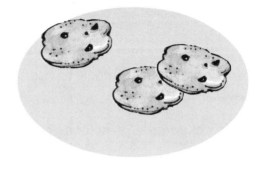

1. Can _____ make some cookies?

2. It is time for _____ to go to practice.

3. It was fun for _____ to sleep in the tent.

4. _____ have a new kitten.

Write a sentence using we.

_____

Write a sentence using us.

_____

MATH TIME

Find the answers.

3(4) =	7(8) =	5(6) =	9(2) =	10(8) =	72(2) =
12(6) =	10(10) =	25(1) =	4(9) =	8(3) =	51(3) =
2(7) =	6(5) =	11(4) =	12(12) =	11(9) =	36(0) =

Week 9

Wednesday

Ge✦graphy

Using this map, give specific directions for traveling from the Oxley Nature Center to the Philbrook Museum of Art.

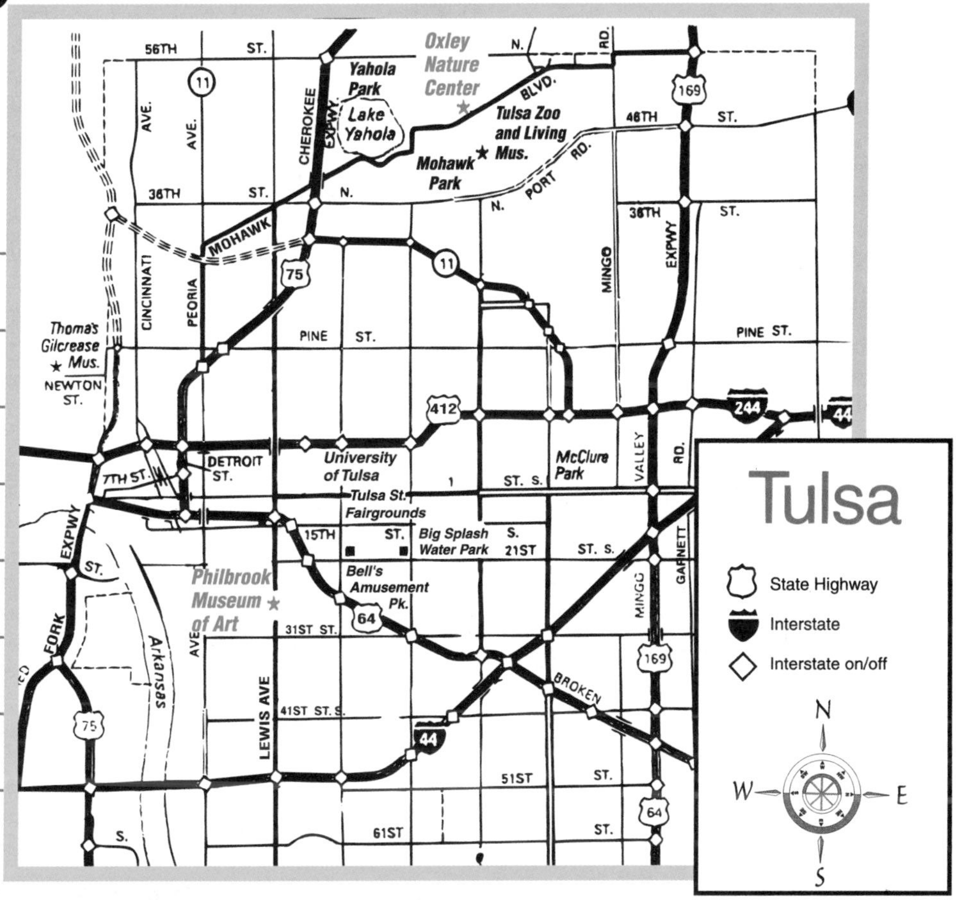

_____

_____

_____

_____

_____

_____

_____

_____

Tulsa

⬡ State Highway

🛡 Interstate

◇ Interstate on/off

N
W — E
S

In My Own Words...
Impossible!

Write about something people thought was impossible in the past.

_____

Write about something you did that you thought was impossible.

_____

Write about something you think is impossible now but might be possible in the future.

_____

_____

Thursday

Week 9

113

Language Lines

Use can or may in each sentence.

May I?

1. _____ I please go to Tori's party?

2. Chelsea runs so fast, she _____ always score a goal.

3. Yvette _____ make a birdhouse without any help.

4. I _____ carry all the groceries inside.

5. You _____ not bring your radio to the dinner table.

Write a sentence using can.

_____

Write a sentence using may.

_____

MATH TIME

Choose the correct answers.

1. A baby weighed 8 lb., 3 oz. at birth. At age 3 months, the baby weighed 12 lb., 5 oz. How much weight did the baby gain in three months?

   (a) 4 lb., 2 oz.   (b) 5 lb.   (c) 4 lb., 9 oz

2. The wheelbarrow weighed 30 kilograms when it was full of sand. When empty, it weighed 12 kilograms, 25 grams. How much sand does it hold?

   (a) 18 kilograms   (b) 17 kilograms, 75 grams   (c) 17 kilograms, 975 grams

3. The recipe calls for 3 cups of juice to make enough punch for 6 people. How much juice is needed to make punch for one dozen people?

   (a) 5 cups   (b) 1 quart, 2 cups   (c) 1 quart, 3 cups

Circle the verb that completes each sentence.

1. They _____ the game carefully.

2. Mystery stories _____ exciting.

3. My hen _____ eggs in the nest.

4. The girls _____ beautifully.

play	plays
is	are
lay	lays
dance	dances

Write a sentence about a helicopter.

_____

Write a sentence about four snails.

_____

MATH TIME

Find the answers.

1. How many feet are in three yards?

_____

2. How many inches are in two feet?

_____

3. How many inches are in one yard?

_____

4. How many feet are in fifty yards?

_____

Friday

Week 9

Complete these analogies.

Analogies

1. Wall is to brick as skeleton is to _____.
   foot, legs, bone, skin

2. Sail is to boat as engine is to _____.
   truck, battery, drive, bicycle

3. Hand is to mitten as head is to _____.
   arm, coat, hat, hair

4. Tall is to short as night is to _____.
   twilight, dark, long, day

5. Flashlight is to light as furnace is to _____.
   ice, winter, night, heat

6. Camel is to desert as ship is to _____.
   sand, vehicle, ocean, passenger

7. Closet is to clothes as refrigerator is to _____.
   house, food, ice cream, kitchen

Write two analogies of your own.

_____

_____

Week 9   Friday

Color a for each page finished.

Parent's Initials

Monday ☆☆ _____

Tuesday ☆☆ _____

Wednesday ☆☆ _____

Thursday ☆☆ _____

Friday ☆☆ _____

Spelling Words

happiness	fearful
worthless	harmful
useless	quietly
smartest	quickly
kindest	happiest
largest	busiest

A Memorable Moment

What sticks in your mind about this week? Write about it.

_____

_____

_____

_____

Keeping Track

Color a book for every 15 minutes you read.

Monday	Tuesday	Wednesday	Thursday	Friday

Could the events in the book you are reading really happen? Explain.

_____

_____

_____

Farming with Worms

Worms are good composters. They eat organic waste and turn it into soil. Start your own worm farm, and soon you will reduce the amount of organic trash that you throw away.

Your worm farm container should be about the size of a bag of groceries. Experienced worm farmers believe that wood makes the best worm farm container. Drill holes in the bottom of the container for drainage and air circulation. Make one hole every 3 to 4 inches. Set the container on bricks so the air can get into the box through the holes. Your container will need a plastic cover just a little smaller than the top of the container.

Tear old newspaper into strips about an inch wide. Soak the newspaper strips in water until they are soggy. Put a layer of soggy strips in the box. Add several handfuls of soil and mix. Your farm is ready for worms. Add a pound of red wigglers. (That's about 1,000 worms!) You can buy them at a feed store or a bait shop.

In a few days, you will need to feed your worms. Lift the plastic cover. Add a few scraps of food. Cover the scraps with 2 to 3 inches of soggy newspaper strips. Put the plastic top back in place.

Your worm farm is a miniature compost pile.

1. Why are worm farms valuable?

_____

_____

2. What materials are needed to build a worm farm?

_____

_____

3. What does the phrase "Worms are good composters" mean?

_____

_____

4. What evidence can you find in the story to support the idea that worms don't weigh very much?

_____

1. did you see the rattlesnake special on pbs i seen it twice

_____

_____

2. me and my family is visiting orlando florida for an week said dr luiz

_____

_____

3. the clown selected marco my oldest brother two be her helper

_____

_____

MATH TIME

Find the answers.

1. During the soccer season, Rosa scored at least one point in half of her games. If she played 8 games, in how many games did Rosa score? _____

2. Andy is baking muffins for breakfast. Each box makes 8 muffins. If he wants to make at least 30 muffins, how many boxes will he need to use? _____

3. Kane's desk has three drawers in it. In each drawer he has 12 puzzles. How many puzzles does he have in all? _____

Week 10

Monday

Spell It!

ful	ly	est	less

1. use _____ _____

2. quick _____ _____

3. busy _____ _____

4. large _____ _____

5. worth _____

6. quiet _____ _____

7. harm _____ _____

8. smart _____ _____

9. kind _____ _____

Copy this paragraph in your best handwriting.

Handwriting

The Water Cycle

Hot sun warms the Earth and causes water to evaporate. When the water vapor rises up into the sky, it meets cold air and condenses into droplets. Millions of drops join to make clouds. When a cloud is full, waterdrops fall back to Earth.

Language Lines

Add es to each verb. You may have to change y to an i first.

rush _____   fry_____   mix_____   buzz_____

Fill in the missing verb in each sentence.

1. Mr. Evans _____ to catch the bus.

2. Mom _____ the bacon for my sandwich.

3. The bee _____ around the jam jar.

MATH⏱TIME

Write the correct letter(s) to describe each pair of lines.

a = parallel   b = perpendicular   c = intersecting

_____ //   _____ ⋋   _____ +

_____ ✕   _____ †   _____ ⫽

Week 10

Tuesday

The Farming Business

In many parts of the world, farming is a very big business. Farmers need to know much more than how to plant a seed. They need to know how to plan ahead, how machines work, what soil conditions make plants grow well, and how to keep track of money.

To plan their farming year, farmers must know what crops people will buy. They study government reports and other materials to decide what to grow each year.

Some crops require specific kinds of machines to plant, cultivate, or harvest them. The farmer must decide which machines to buy or rent each year. The machinery is purchased or rented with the money from last year's crops.

Some crops require special kinds of soil to grow well. The farmer must study the chemistry of the soil and plan how to make the soil best for the crops. Sometimes fertilizer or chemicals must be purchased to improve the soil.

All this planning requires money. The farmer must keep close track of the money earned by selling the crops. Each year money must be spent on machinery, soil conditioners, and, of course, seed. The farmer must be a good money manager to have a successful farm.

A farmer must combine knowledge of many different occupations to be successful. Explain how a farmer is like:

a scientist _____

_____

a mechanic _____

_____

a fortune-teller _____

_____

a weather forecaster _____

_____

an accountant _____

_____

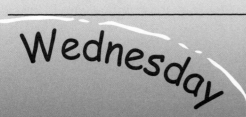

Wednesday

Week 10

An adverb tells how, when, or where.

Circle the adverb that tells about each underlined verb.
Then write how, when, or where to tell how the adverb is used.

1. Annie <u>sang</u> quietly to her little sister. _____

2. Carlos <u>practiced</u> ball yesterday. _____

3. When I dropped the box, the cereal <u>flew</u> everywhere. _____

4. The boy <u>waited</u> patiently for his turn. _____

MATH ⏰ TIME

Write the answers.

1. Label each angle: right, obtuse, acute.

_____   _____   _____

2. Match the congruent figures.

Explain what congruent means.

_____

_____

Geography

1. How many countries are labeled on this map? _____

2. Which country is the largest? _____

3. Which Asian capital
   is the farthest...

east? _____

west? _____

south? _____

north? _____

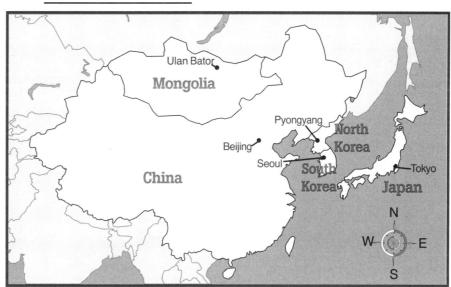

In My Own Words...

Make a list of three questions that you would answer "Yes."

_____

_____

_____

Make a list of three questions that you would answer "No."

_____

_____

_____

1. The girls _____ so busy fishing, they forgot the time. "I'm getting hungry," announced Cherrie.

2. Cindy _____ ready for a snack too. "The sandwiches _____ in that sack. There _____ some cookies too," she said.

3. "_____ there anything to drink?" asked Cherrie.

4. "The juice _____ in the thermos over there," answered Cindy.

Find the answers.

1. Larry painted his birdhouse from 3:45 p.m. until 5:00 p.m. How long did he work? _____

2. Clara's new watch is guaranteed for 90 days. About how many months is that? _____

3. Tasha bought some new clothes. The total of her purchase was $72.27. If she gave the clerk $80, how much money did she get back? _____

Language Lines

Write the correct punctuation at the end of each sentence. Then tell which type it is.

A statement tells something.

A question asks something.

An exclamation shows strong feeling.

1. What time do we have swim lessons _____

2. Let's meet at the pool _____

3. Your wet suit will ruin the rug _____

4. Swimming is hard work _____

5. Can you help me do it _____

MATH TIME

Find the answers.

1. What are the common factors of 16 and 24? _____

2. What are the first three common multiples of 6 and 8? _____

3. Match each number to its set of multiples.

6		10, 15, 20, 25, 30
5		12, 18, 24, 30, 36
8		16, 24, 32, 40, 48

4. Give all the factors of 8. _____

The Starting Line

Ten students are in the final round of the Spelling Bee. For the newspaper photo, they lined up in order from tallest to shortest. Name the spellers in the photograph.

1. Amber is standing next to Carlos.

2. Hoa is just taller than Jamal, who is standing next to Maria, who is shorter.

3. Carlos is the tallest person.

4. Raul is taller than Maria, and they are both taller than Victor.

5. No one is standing between Raul (the taller) and Yasmin.

6. No one is standing between Fran and Amber.

7. Yasmin is shorter than Olga, who is just shorter than Fran.

8. Olga is taller than Raul, who is taller than Hoa. They are all taller than Maria.

Answer Key

Checking your child's work is an important part of learning. It allows you to see what your child knows well and what areas need more practice. It also provides an opportunity for you to help your child understand that making mistakes is a part of learning.

When an error is discovered, ask your child to look carefully at the question or problem. Errors often occur through misreading the problem. Your child can quickly correct these errors.

The answer key pages can be used in several ways:

- Remove the answer pages and give the book to your child. Go over the answers with him or her as each day's work is completed.

- Leave the answer pages in the book and give the practice pages to your child one day at a time.

- Leave the answer pages in the book so your child can check his or her own answers as the pages are completed. It is still important that you review the pages with your child if you use this method.

Page 11

Page 12

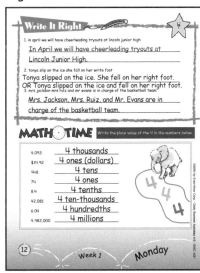

Page 13

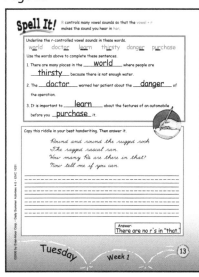

Page 14

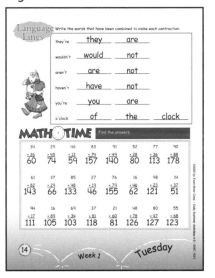

Page 15

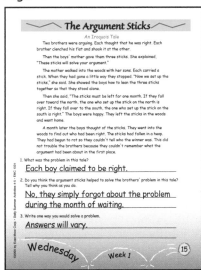

Page 16

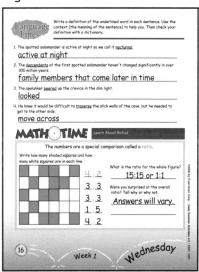

Page 17

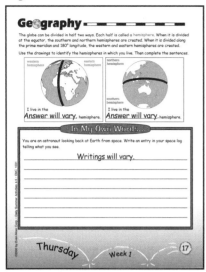

Geography

The globe can be divided in half two ways. Each half is called a hemisphere. When it is divided at the equator, the southern and northern hemispheres are created. When it is divided along the prime meridian and 180° longitude, the western and eastern hemispheres are created.

Use the drawings to identify the hemispheres in which you live. Then complete the sentences.

western hemisphere / eastern hemisphere

I live in the **Answer will vary.** hemisphere.

northern hemisphere / southern hemisphere

I live in the **Answer will vary.** hemisphere.

In My Own Words....

You are an astronaut looking back at Earth from space. Write an entry in your space log telling what you see.

Writings will vary.

Thursday — Week 1 — (17)

Page 18

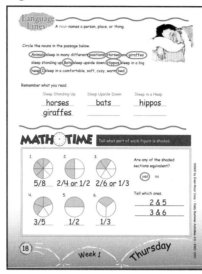

Language Lines

A noun names a person, place, or thing.

Circle the nouns in the passage below.

(Animals) sleep in many different (positions). (Horses) and (giraffes) sleep standing up. (Bats) sleep upside down. (Hippos) sleep in a big (heap). (I) sleep in a comfortable, soft, cozy, warm (bed).

Remember what you read.

Sleep Standing Up	Sleep Upside Down	Sleep in a Heap
horses giraffes	bats	hippos

MATH TIME — Tell what part of each figure is shaded.

1. 5/8 2. 2/4 or 1/2 3. 2/6 or 1/3

Are any of the shaded sections equivalent? **yes** no

4. 3/5 5. 1/2 6. 1/3

Tell which ones. **2 & 5 3 & 6**

(18) — Week 1 — Thursday

Page 19

Language Lines

Write these words in alphabetical order. **A B C**

turn, duck, whistle, eagle, Relax!, hawk, zip, juniper, lupine, Nice!, grouse, yell, maple, Perfect!, apples, Quiet!, falcon, ivy, Shush!, bananas, unpack, vote, cherries, Ouch!, kudzu

apples	falcon	kudzu	Perfect!	unpack
bananas	grouse	lupine	Quite!	vote
cherries	hawk	maple	Relax!	whistle
duck	ivy	Nice!	Shush!	yell
eagle	juniper	Ouch!	turn	zip

The list above can be divided into five categories. Color the boxes in each category a different color.

MATH TIME — Find the answers.

1. Thomas is saving money to buy a game cartridge. The cartridge costs $24.95. If he has $12.50, how much more money does Thomas need? **$12.45**

2. Sally's dog had six puppies. If Sally keeps one puppy for herself and sells the others for $12 each, how much money will she earn? **$60**

3. Dave has five more chickens than he has dogs. He has one less cat than he has dogs. If he has three dogs, how many pets does he have? **13 pets**

Friday — Week 1 — (19)

Page 20

Whose Tree?

Each state in the United States has chosen a special tree to represent their state. Use the clues and the matrix to match the following states and their trees. Write yes to show a correct answer. Make an X to show incorrect answers.

- Rhode Island's tree is two words. The first letter of the first word for the state and the tree are the same.
- California's tree is named for the color of its trunk.
- The American elm is not the state tree of Florida, Nevada, or Georgia.
- Oregon's tree is a popular Christmas tree that begins with a person's name.
- The name of South Carolina's tree begins with the same letter as the state.
- The single-leaf piñon tree represents a state that borders California.

	redwood	single-leaf piñon	American elm	live oak	Douglas fir	Sabal palmetto	red maple
Oregon	X	X	X	X	yes	X	X
Massachusetts & N. Dakota	X	X	yes	X	X	X	X
Rhode Island	X	X	X	X	X	X	yes
California	yes	X	X	X	X	X	X
Florida & S. Carolina	X	X	X	X	X	yes	X
Nevada	X	yes	X	X	X	X	X
Georgia	X	X	X	yes	X	X	X

(20) — Week 1 — Friday

Page 23

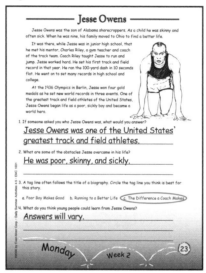

Jesse Owens

Jesse Owens was the son of Alabama sharecroppers. As a child he was skinny and often sick. When he was nine, his family moved to Ohio to find a better life.

It was there, while Jesse was in junior high school, that he met his mentor, Charles Riley, a gym teacher and coach of the track team. Coach Riley taught Jesse to run and jump. Jesse worked hard. He set his first track and field record in that year. He ran the 100-yard dash in 10 seconds flat. He went on to set many records in high school and college.

At the 1936 Olympics in Berlin, Jesse won four gold medals as he set new world records in three events. One of the greatest track and field athletes of the United States, Jesse Owens began life as a poor, sickly boy and became a world hero.

1. If someone asked you who Jesse Owens was, what would you answer?
Jesse Owens was one of the United States' greatest track and field athletes.

2. What are some of the obstacles Jesse overcame in his life?
He was poor, skinny, and sickly.

3. A tag line often follows the title of a biography. Circle the tag line you think is best for this story.
a. Poor Boy Makes Good   b. Running to a Better Life   **c. The Difference a Coach Makes**

4. What do you think young people could learn from Jesse Owens?
Answers will vary.

Monday — Week 2 — (23)

Page 24

Language Lines

1. ben taked pictures of the team for boy's life magazine
Ben took pictures of the team for Boy's Life magazine.

2. does you like a aluminum bat or a wooden one
Do you like an aluminum bat or a wooden one?

3. mom said we needs to stop to bye gas before we leave for bass lake
Mom said, "We need to stop to buy gas before we leave for Bass Lake."

MATH TIME — Find the answers.

96	24	81	75	39	48	52	63	17	80
-62	-18	-56	-26	-22	-39	-47	-60	-13	-74
34	6	25	49	17	9	5	3	4	6

25	90	31	67	42	79	86	59	68	31
-18	-73	-22	-48	-35	-49	-59	-31	-65	-17
7	17	9	19	7	30	27	28	3	14

83	27	75	46	53	11	37	94	52	61
-59	-18	-58	-27	-44	-10	-29	-78	-36	-45
24	9	17	19	9	1	8	16	16	16

(24) — Week 2 — Monday

Page 25

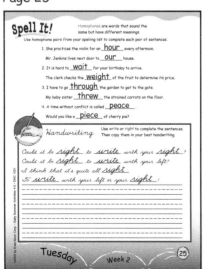

Spell It!

Homophones are words that sound the same but have different meanings.

Use homophone pairs from your spelling list to complete each pair of sentences.

1. She practices the violin for an **hour** every afternoon.
Mr. Jenkins lives next door to **our** house.

2. It is hard to **wait** for your birthday to arrive.
The clerk checks the **weight** of the fruit to determine its price.

3. I have to go **through** the garden to get to the gate.
My baby sister **threw** the strained carrots on the floor.

4. A time without conflict is called **peace**.
Would you like a **piece** of cherry pie?

Handwriting

Use write or right to complete the sentences. Then copy them in your best handwriting.

Could it be **right** to **write** with your **right**?
Could it be **right** to **write** with your left?
I think that it's quite all **right**.
To **write** with your left or your **right**!

Tuesday — Week 2 — (25)

Page 26

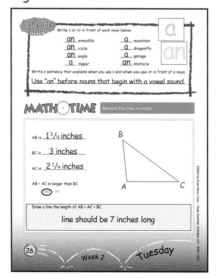

Language Lines

Write a or an in front of each noun below.

an armadillo   **a** mountain
an icicle   **a** dragonfly
an eagle   **a** garage
a zipper   **an** obstacle

a / an

Write a sentence that explains when you use a and when you use an in front of a noun.
Use "an" before nouns that begin with a vowel sound.

MATH TIME — Measure the lines in inches.

AB is **1 3/4 inches**
BC is **3 inches**
AC is **2 1/4 inches**

AB + AC is longer than BC. **yes** no

Draw a line the length of AB + AC + BC.
line should be 7 inches long

(26) — Week 2 — Tuesday

Page 27

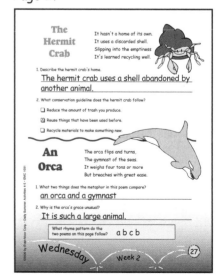

The Hermit Crab

It hasn't a home of its own.
It uses a discarded shell.
Slipping into the emptiness
It's learned recycling well.

1. Describe the hermit crab's home.
The hermit crab uses a shell abandoned by another animal.

2. What conservation guideline does the hermit crab follow?
☐ Reduce the amount of trash you produce.
☑ Reuse things that have been used before.
☐ Recycle materials to make something new.

An Orca

The orca flips and turns,
The gymnast of the sea.
It weighs four tons or more
But breaches with great ease.

1. What two things does the metaphor in this poem compare?
an orca and a gymnast

2. Why is the orca's grace unusual?
It is such a large animal.

What rhyme pattern do the two poems on this page follow? **a b c b**

Wednesday — Week 2 — (27)

Page 28

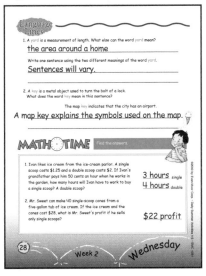

Language Lines

1. A *yard* is a measurement of length. What else can the word *yard* mean?

the area around a home

Write one sentence using the two different meanings of the word *yard*.

Sentences will vary.

2. A *key* is a metal object used to turn the bolt of a lock. What does the word *key* mean in this sentence?

The map *key* indicates that the city has an airport.

A map key explains the symbols used on the map.

MATH TIME — Find the answers.

1. Ivan likes ice cream from the ice-cream parlor. A single scoop costs $1.25 and a double scoop costs $2. If Ivan's grandfather pays him 50 cents an hour when he works in the garden, how many hours will Ivan have to work to buy a single scoop? A double scoop?

3 hours single
4 hours double

2. Mr. Sweet can make 40 single-scoop cones from a five-gallon tub of ice cream. If the ice cream and the cones cost $28, what is his profit if he sells only single scoops?

$22 profit

(28) Week 2 Wednesday

Page 29

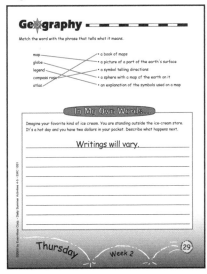

Geography

Match the word with the phrase that tells what it means.

map — a book of maps
globe — a picture of a part of the earth's surface
legend — a symbol telling directions
compass rose — a sphere with a map of the earth on it
atlas — an explanation of the symbols used on a map

In My Own Words....

Imagine your favorite kind of ice cream. You are standing outside the ice-cream store. It's a hot day and you have two dollars in your pocket. Describe what happens next.

Writings will vary.

Thursday Week 2 (29)

Page 30

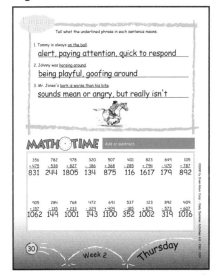

Language Lines

Tell what the underlined phrase in each sentence means.

1. Tommy is always *on the ball.*

alert, paying attention, quick to respond

2. Johnny was *horsing around.*

being playful, goofing around

3. Mr. Jones's *bark is worse than his bite.*

sounds mean or angry, but really isn't

MATH TIME — Add or subtract.

356	782	978	320	507	401	823	649	105
+475	-538	+827	-186	+368	-285	+794	-470	+787
831	244	1805	134	875	116	1617	179	892

905	284	768	472	691	537	123	892	409
+157	-135	+233	-329	+409	-185	+879	-573	+607
1062	149	1001	143	1100	352	1002	319	1016

(30) Week 2 Thursday

Page 31

Language Lines

Use pairs of rhyming words to answer the questions. You will find one-half of each pair in the word box.

Word Box

red	big	flat	green	lucky	marriage

1. What do you call someone whose hair is the color of a tomato? **redhead**
2. What do you call a large hog? **big pig**
3. What do you call a cap after an elephant sits on it? **flat hat**
4. What do you call a grass-colored vegetable? **green bean**
5. What do you call a web-footed winner? **lucky duck**
6. What do you call a wagon used by the bride and groom? **marriage carriage**

MATH TIME — Pete's Bugs

Pete collects bugs and keeps them in a cage. Once a week he opens the lid to add 5 new bugs. Each time he does, 3 bugs get away. If he starts with 18 bugs, how many bugs will he have at the end of six weeks? **30**

Complete this table to find the answer to the question.

	WEEK 1	WEEK 2	WEEK 3	WEEK 4	WEEK 5	WEEK 6
Beginning of Week	18	20	22	24	26	28
Bugs In	5	5	5	5	5	5
Bugs Out	3	3	3	3	3	3
End of Week	20	22	24	26	28	30

Friday Week 2 (31)

Page 32

Magic Squares

Fill in each magic square. Use the numerals 1 through 9. Use each number only once per square. The numbers must total 15 when they are added together horizontally and vertically. Give three different solutions.

3 possible solutions are shown.

9	2	4
1	6	8
5	7	3

2	7	6
4	3	8
9	5	1

5	9	1
7	2	6
3	4	8

On another sheet of paper, create your own magic square puzzle.

(32) Week 2 Friday

Page 35

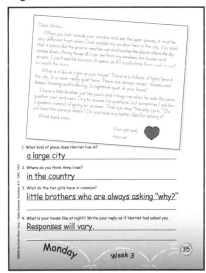

Dear Anna,

When you look outside your window and see the open spaces, it must be very different from when I look outside my window here in the city. You said that it seems like the prairie reaches out and touches the places where the sky comes down. At my house all I can see from my window are houses and streets. I can't see the horizon. It seems as if I could climb from roof to roof to reach the stars.

What is it like at night at your house? There are millions of lights here in the city. It is never really quiet here. There are always noises—buzzes and beeps, honking and hollering. Is nighttime quiet at your house?

I have a little brother just like yours and it bugs me when he asks the same question over and over. I try to answer his questions, but sometimes I ask him a question instead of giving an answer. That can stop "the why cycle." Do you have the same problem? Do you have any better idea for solving it?

Write back soon.

Your pen pal,
Harriet

1. What kind of place does Harriet live in?
a large city

2. Where do you think Anna lives?
in the country

3. What do these two girls have in common?
little brothers who are always asking "why?"

4. What is your house like at night? Write your reply as if Harriet had asked you.
Responses will vary.

Monday Week 3 (35)

Page 36

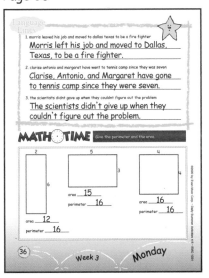

Language Lines

1. morris leaved his job and moved to dallas texas to be a fire fighter

Morris left his job and moved to Dallas, Texas, to be a fire fighter.

2. clarise antonio and margaret have went to tennis camp since they was seven

Clarise, Antonio, and Margaret have gone to tennis camp since they were seven.

3. the scientists didnt give up when they couldnt figure out the problem

The scientists didn't give up when they couldn't figure out the problem.

MATH TIME — Give the perimeter and the area.

area **15**
perimeter **16**

area **16**
perimeter **16**

area **12**
perimeter **16**

(36) Week 3 Monday

Page 37

Spell It!

Write the words that combine to form each of the following words. Then write a sentence using the two words, explaining each compound word.

breakfast   break + fast

You break your nightlong fast when you eat breakfast.

1. earthquake **earth** + **quake**
Sentences will vary.
2. headache **head** + **ache**
3. lifeguard **life** + **guard**
4. wristwatch **wrist** + **watch**

Handwriting

Copy these words.
skyscraper
everybody
everywhere

Copy these words.
Yolanda
Yesterday
Yemen

Tuesday Week 3 (37)

Page 38

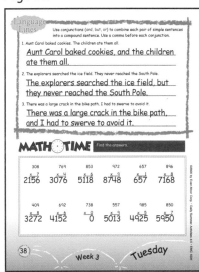

Language Lines

Use conjunctions (and, but, or) to combine each pair of simple sentences into a compound sentence. Use a comma before each conjunction.

1. Aunt Carol baked cookies. The children ate them all.
Aunt Carol baked cookies, and the children ate them all.

2. The explorers searched the ice field. They never reached the South Pole.
The explorers searched the ice field, but they never reached the South Pole.

3. There was a large crack in the bike path. I had to swerve to avoid it.
There was a large crack in the bike path, and I had to swerve to avoid it.

MATH TIME — Find the answers.

308	769	853	972	657	896
x 7	x 4	x 6	x 9	x 1	x 8
2156	3076	5118	8748	657	7168

409	692	738	557	985	850
x 8	x 6	x 0	x 9	x 5	x 7
3272	4152	0	5013	4925	5950

(38) Week 3 Tuesday

Page 39

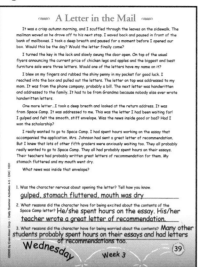

A Letter in the Mail

It was a crisp autumn morning, and I scuffled through the leaves on the sidewalk. The mailman waved as he drove off to his next stop. I waved back and paused in front of the bank of mailboxes. I took a deep breath and paused for a moment before I opened our box. Would this be the day? Would the letter finally come?

I turned the key in the lock and slowly swung the door open. On top of the usual flyers announcing the current price of chicken legs and apples and the biggest and best furniture sale were three letters. Would one of the letters have my name on it?

I blew on my fingers and rubbed the shiny penny in my pocket for good luck. I reached into the box and pulled out the letters. The letter on top was addressed to my mom. It was from the phone company, probably a bill. The next letter was handwritten and addressed to the family. It had to be from Grandma because nobody else wrote handwritten letters.

One more letter...I took a deep breath and looked at the return address. It was from Space Camp. It was addressed to me. This was the letter I had been waiting for! I gulped and felt the smooth, stiff envelope. Was the news inside good or bad? Had I won the scholarship?

I really wanted to go to Space Camp. I had spent hours working on the essay that accompanied the application. Mrs. Johnson had sent a great letter of recommendation. But I knew that lots of other fifth graders were anxiously waiting too. They all probably really wanted to go to Space Camp. They all had probably spent hours on their essays. Their teachers had probably written great letters of recommendation for them. My stomach fluttered and my mouth went dry.

What news was inside that envelope?

1. Was the character nervous about opening the letter? Tell how you know.
gulped, stomach fluttered, mouth was dry

2. What reasons did the character have for being excited about the contents of the Space Camp letter? He/she spent hours on the essay. His/her teacher wrote a great letter of recommendation.

3. What reasons did the character have for being worried about the contents? Many other students probably spent hours on their essays and had letters of recommendations too.

Wednesday   Week 3   (39)

Page 40

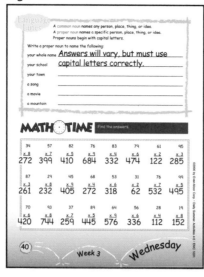

A common noun names any person, place, thing, or idea.
A proper noun names a specific person, place, thing, or idea.
Proper nouns begin with capital letters.

Write a proper noun to name the following:

your whole name **Answers will vary, but must use capital letters correctly.**

your school ____

your town ____

a song ____

a movie ____

a mountain ____

MATH TIME — Find the answers.

34 ×8	57 ×7	82 ×5	76 ×9	83 ×4	79 ×6	61 ×2	95 ×3
272	399	410	684	332	474	122	285
87 ×3	29 ×8	45 ×9	68 ×4	53 ×6	31 ×2	76 ×7	99 ×5
261	232	405	272	318	62	532	495
70 ×6	93 ×8	37 ×7	89 ×5	64 ×9	56 ×6	28 ×4	19 ×8
420	744	259	445	576	336	112	152

(40)   Week 3   Wednesday

Page 41

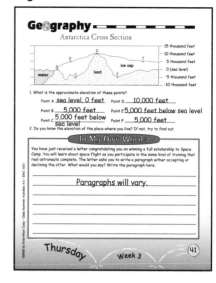

Geography
Antarctica Cross Section

1. What is the approximate elevation of these points?
Point A **sea level, 0 feet**   Point D **10,000 feet**
Point B **5,000 feet**   Point E **5,000 feet below sea level**
Point C **5,000 feet below sea level**   Point F **5,000 feet**

2. Do you know the elevation of the place where you live? If not, try to find out.

In My Own Words....

You have just received a letter congratulating you on winning a full scholarship to Space Camp. You will learn about space flight as you participate in the same kind of training that real astronauts complete. The letter asks you to write a paragraph either accepting or declining the offer. What would you say? Write the paragraph here.

Paragraphs will vary.

Thursday   Week 3   (41)

Page 42

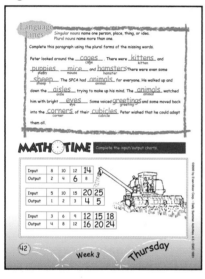

Singular nouns name one person, place, thing, or idea.
Plural nouns name more than one.

Complete this paragraph using the plural forms of the missing words.

Peter looked around the **cages**. There were **kittens** and **puppies**, **mice**, and **hamsters**. There were even some **sheep**. The SPCA had **animals** for everyone. He walked up and down the **aisles** trying to make up his mind. The **animals** watched him with bright **eyes**. Some voiced **greetings** and some moved back into the **corners** of their **cubicles**. Peter wished that he could adopt them all.

MATH TIME — Complete the input/output charts.

Input	8	10	12	14
Output	2	4	6	8

Input	5	10	15	20	25
Output	1	2	3	4	5

Input	3	6	9	12	15	18
Output	4	8	12	16	20	24

(42)   Week 3   Thursday

Page 43

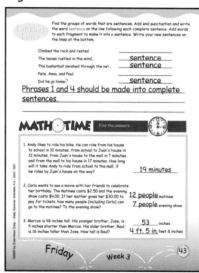

Find the groups of words that are sentences. Add end punctuation and write the word *sentence* on the line following each complete sentence. Add words to each fragment to make it into a sentence. Write your new sentences on the lines at the bottom.

Climbed the rock and rested ____
The leaves rustled in the wind. **sentence**
The basketball swished through the net. **sentence**
Pete, Anna, and Paul ____
Did he go home? **sentence**

Phrases 1 and 4 should be made into complete sentences.

MATH TIME — Find the answers.

1. Andy likes to ride his bike. He can ride from his house to school in 10 minutes, from school to Juan's house in 12 minutes, from Juan's house to the mall in 7 minutes, and from the mall to his house in 17 minutes. How long will it take Andy to ride from school to the mall, if he rides by Juan's house on the way?   **19 minutes**

2. Carla wants to see a movie with her friends to celebrate her birthday. The matinee costs $2.50 and the evening show costs $4.00. If her mother gives her $30.00 to pay for tickets, how many people (including Carla) can go to the matinee? To the evening show?   **12 people** matinee **7 people** evening show

3. Marcos is 48 inches tall. His younger brother, Jose, is 9 inches shorter than Marcos. His older brother, Raul, is 16 inches taller than Jose. How tall is Raul?   **53** inches **4 ft. 5 in.** feet & inches

Friday   Week 3   (43)

Page 44

Buried Treasure

Here are the directions for pacing the way to the buried treasure. Shade in the squares as you go.

You are here!

1. Four paces south
2. Six paces west
3. Three paces south
4. Two paces west
5. Eight paces south
6. Five paces east
7. Seven paces north
8. One step east
9. Three paces north
10. Dig!

What do you think you will find?
Answers will vary.

(44)   Week 3   Friday

Page 47

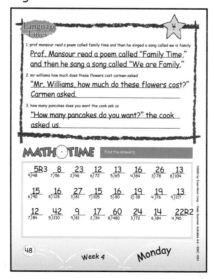

Allen Say

Allen Say was born in Yokohama, Japan. When he was six years old, he decided that he wanted to be a cartoonist. However, the world was at war. In the midst of the war, he attended seven different elementary schools. When the war ended, Allen was sent to live with his grandmother. She didn't get along with him, so he was allowed to live alone until he was twelve. At age twelve he apprenticed himself to a famous Japanese cartoonist, Noro Shinpei.

He spent the next four years drawing and painting.

When Allen was sixteen, his father moved with Allen to the United States. Allen went to a military school in California for one year and then struck out on his own. He moved from job to job, city to city, and school to school. He painted his way through California before he opened a photography studio.

Today Allen Say is a successful writer, illustrator, and photographer. Many of his books tell about parts of his life. His autobiographical story, *Grandfather's Journey*, won the Caldecott Medal in 1993. He says that it is a joyous experience to tell a story with his brush.

1. What was Allen Say's ambition?
to be a cartoonist

2. What was unusual about young Allen's life?
He lived on his own before the age of 12.

3. What does it mean to "apprentice oneself to another person"?
to work for a master in order to learn a skill

4. What do you do that is a joyous experience?
Answers will vary.

Check in your public library for a book written by Allen Say. *The Apprentice's Ink* is a chapter book that tells about his time as an apprentice.

Monday   Week 4   (47)

Page 48

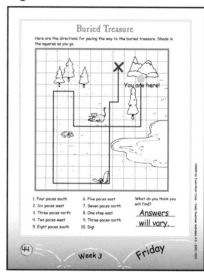

1. prof mansour read a poem called family time and then he singed a song called we are family
Prof. Mansour read a poem called "Family Time," and then he sang a song called "We are Family."

2. mr williams how much do these flowers cost carmen asked
"Mr. Williams, how much do these flowers cost?" Carmen asked.

3. how many pancakes does you want the cook ask us
"How many pancakes do you want?" the cook asked us.

MATH TIME — Find the answers.

9)48 **5R3**	7)56 **8**	2)46 **23**	6)72 **12**	5)65 **13**	4)64 **16**	3)78 **26**	8)104 **13**
6)90 **15**	8)128 **16**	7)105 **15**	5)80 **16**	2)38 **19**	4)76 **19**	9)117 **13**
7)84 **12**	5)210 **42**	9)81 **9**	2)34 **17**	8)480 **60**	3)72 **24**	6)84 **14**	4)90 **22R2**

(48)   Week 4   Monday

Page 49

Spell It!

Cross out the silent letter(s) in each of the words below. Then use the words to complete the sentences.

~k~not   ~w~rong   un~k~nown   climbed   neig~h~bor   ~w~hole   lim~b~

1. My **neighbor** rescued my kitten when it **climbed** out on the **limb**.

2. The letter came to the **wrong** address, so I wrote **unknown** on the envelope.

3. Sue's stomach was tied in a **knot** as she got ready to give the speech.

Copy these sentences in your best handwriting.

Marvelous, magnificent Monday.
Totally terrific Tuesday.
Wild and wonderful Wednesday.
Thoroughly thrilling Thursday.
And finally fun-filled Friday.
What a week!

Tuesday   Week 4   (49)

Page 50

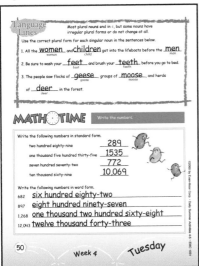

Language Lines

Most plural nouns end in s, but some nouns have irregular plural forms or do not change at all.

Use the correct plural form for each singular noun in the sentences below.

1. All the **women** and **children** got into the lifeboats before the **men**.

2. Be sure to wash your **feet** and brush your **teeth** before you go to bed.

3. The people saw flocks of **geese**, groups of **moose**, and herds of **deer** in the forest.

MATH TIME — Write the numbers.

Write the following numbers in standard form.

two hundred eighty-nine	**289**
one thousand five hundred thirty-five	**1535**
seven hundred seventy-two	**772**
ten thousand sixty-nine	**10,069**

Write the following numbers in word form.

682	**six hundred eighty-two**
897	**eight hundred ninety-seven**
1,268	**one thousand two hundred sixty-eight**
12,043	**twelve thousand forty-three**

50 — Week 4 — Tuesday

Page 51

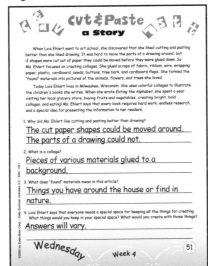

Cut & Paste a Story

When Lois Ehlert went to art school, she discovered that she liked cutting and pasting better than she liked drawing. It was hard to move the parts of a drawing around, but if shapes were cut out of paper they could be moved before they were glued down. So Ms. Ehlert focused on creating collages. She glued scraps of fabric, ribbon, wire, wrapping paper, plastic, cardboard, seeds, buttons, tree bark, and cardboard flaps. She formed the "found" materials into pictures of the animals, flowers, and trees she loved.

Today Lois Ehlert lives in Milwaukee, Wisconsin. She uses colorful collages to illustrate the children's books she writes. When she wrote Eating the Alphabet, she spent a year visiting her local grocery store, buying fruits and vegetables, creating bright, bold collages, and eating! Ms. Ehlert says that every banana requires hard work, endless research, and a special idea for presenting the information to her readers.

1. Why did Ms. Ehlert like cutting and pasting better than drawing?
The cut paper shapes could be moved around.
The parts of a drawing could not.

2. What is a collage?
Pieces of various materials glued to a
background.

3. What does "found" materials mean in this article?
Things you have around the house or find in
nature.

4. Lois Ehlert says that everyone needs a special space for keeping all the things for creating. What things would you keep in your special space? What would you create with those things?
Answers will vary.

Wednesday — Week 4 — 51

Page 52

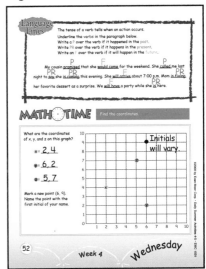

Language Lines

The tense of a verb tells when an action occurs.

Underline the verbs in the paragraph below.
Write a **P** over the verb if it happens in the past.
Write **PR** over the verb if it happens in the present.
Write an **F** over the verb if it will happen in the future.

My cousin _promised_ [PR] that she _would come_ [F] for the weekend. She _called_ [P] me last night to _say_ [PR] she _is coming_ [PR] this evening. She _will arrive_ [F] at 7:00 p.m. Mom _is fixing_ [PR] her favorite dessert as a surprise. We _will have_ [F] a party while she _is_ [PR] here.

MATH TIME — Find the coordinates.

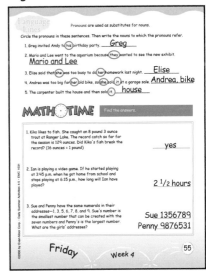

What are the coordinates of x, y, and z on this graph?

x: **2, 4**
y: **6, 2**
z: **5, 7**

Mark a new point (6, 9). Name the point with the first initial of your name.

Initials will vary.

52 — Week 4 — Wednesday

Page 53

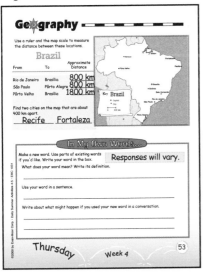

Geography

Use a ruler and the map scale to measure the distance between these locations.

Brazil

From	To	Approximate Distance
Rio de Janeiro	Brasília	**800 km**
São Paulo	Pôrto Alegre	**800 km**
Pôrto Velho	Brasília	**1800 km**

Find two cities on the map that are about 400 km apart.
Recife **Fortaleza**

In My Own Words...

Make a new word. Use parts of existing words if you'd like. Write your word in the box.   **Responses will vary.**

What does your word mean? Write its definition.

Use your word in a sentence.

Write about what might happen if you used your new word in a conversation.

Thursday — Week 4 — 53

Page 54

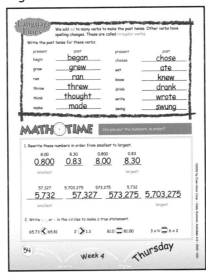

Language Lines

We add ed to many verbs to make the past tense. Other verbs have spelling changes. These are called irregular verbs.

Write the past tense for these verbs.

present	past	present	past
begin	**began**	choose	**chose**
grow	**grew**	eat	**ate**
run	**ran**	know	**knew**
throw	**threw**	drink	**drank**
think	**thought**	write	**wrote**
make	**made**	swing	**swung**

MATH TIME — Can you put the numbers in order?

1. Rewrite these numbers in order from smallest to largest.

8.00   8.30   0.800   0.83
0.800   **0.83**   **8.00**   **8.30**
smallest   largest

57,327   5,703,275   573,275   5,732
5,732   **57,327**   **573,275**   **5,703,275**
smallest   largest

2. Write >, <, or = in the circles to make a true statement.

65.73 (>) 65.81   2 (>) 1.3   81.0 (=) 81.00   3 × 4 (>) 6 × 2

54 — Week 4 — Thursday

Page 55

Language Lines

Pronouns are used as substitutes for nouns.

Circle the pronouns in these sentences. Then write the nouns to which the pronouns refer.

1. Greg invited Andy to his birthday party. **Greg**
2. Mario and Lee went to the aquarium because they wanted to see the new exhibit. **Mario and Lee**
3. Elise said she was too busy to do her homework last night. **Elise**
4. Andrea was too big for her old bike, so she sold it at a garage sale. **Andrea, bike**
5. The carpenter built the house and then sold it. **house**

MATH TIME — Find the answers.

1. Kiko likes to fish. She caught an 8 pound 3 ounce trout at Ranger Lake. The record catch so far for the season is 124 ounces. Did Kiko's fish break the record? (16 ounces = 1 pound)   **yes**

2. Ian is playing a video game. If he started playing at 3:45 p.m. when he got home from school and stops playing at 6:15 p.m., how long will Ian have played?   **2 1/2 hours**

3. Sue and Penny have the same numerals in their addresses—1, 3, 5, 6, 7, 8, and 9. Sue's number is the smallest number that can be created with the seven numbers and Penny's is the largest number. What are the girls' addresses?
Sue 1356789
Penny 9876531

Friday — Week 4 — 55

Page 56

Building Your Vocabulary

Word Box
case, hushed, wish, sienna, skin, sensitive, droned, day, conversation, witnessed, sorrow, dismay, speaks, listened, address, black, broken, special, peels

Crossword answers:
B R O K E N — S P E C I A L
A D D R E S S — S O R R O W
D A Y — S E N S I T I V E
S I E N N A
H U S H E D

Across
1. unusual, out of the ordinary
4. not whole, in pieces
6. to speak to
8. talks
9. great sadness
11. 24-hour period
12. greatly affected by conditions
15. shade of brown
16. quiet, low in volume

Down
2. pulls back to remove
3. talk between people
4. opposite of white
5. paid attention in order to hear
7. frightened amazement
10. saw or observed in person
11. spoke in a dull, monotonous tone
13. outer covering
14. desire, hope
16. evidence or argument for

56 — Week 4 — Friday

Page 59

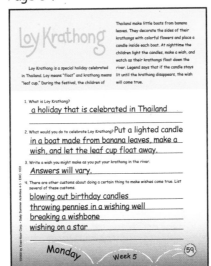

Loy Krathong

Loy Krathong is a special holiday celebrated in Thailand. Loy means "float" and krathong means "leaf cup." During the festival, the children of Thailand make little boats from banana leaves. They decorate the sides of their krathongs with colorful flowers and place a candle inside each boat. At nighttime the children light the candles, make a wish, and watch as their krathongs float down the river. Legend says that if the candle stays lit until the krathong disappears, the wish will come true.

1. What is Loy Krathong?
a holiday that is celebrated in Thailand

2. What would you do to celebrate Loy Krathong? **Put a lighted candle in a boat made from banana leaves, make a wish, and let the leaf cup float away.**

3. Write a wish you might make as you put your krathong in the river.
Answers will vary.

4. There are other customs about doing a certain thing to make wishes come true. List several of these customs.
blowing out birthday candles
throwing pennies in a wishing well
breaking a wishbone
wishing on a star

Monday — Week 5 — 59

Page 60

Language Lines

1. the twins are to write thank-you notes for there birthday presents
The twins have to write thank-you notes
for their birthday presents.

2. how many books did you read this summer asked miss gonzales
"How many books did you read this summer?"
asked Miss Gonzales.

3. i just finished reading harriet the spy anita told henry
"I just finished reading Harriet the Spy,"
Anita told Henry.

MATH TIME — Find the answers.

584 +392 **976**	467 -232 **235**	738 +295 **1033**	197 -126 **71**	625 +316 **941**	393 -204 **189**
37 ×9 **333**	41 ×8 **328**	96 ×6 **576**	27 ×7 **189**	58 ×5 **290**	41 ×9 **369**
8)640 **80**	7)497 **71**	9)828 **92**	6)564 **94**		

60 — Week 5 — Monday

Page 61

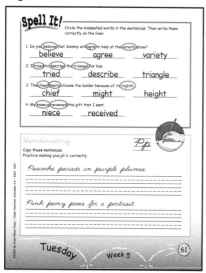

Spell It!
Circle the misspelled words in the sentences. Then write them correctly on the lines.

1. Do you believe that Sammy will agree to help at the variety show?

believe   agree   variety

2. I tried to describe the triangle for him.

tried   describe   triangle

3. The chief might choose the ladder because of its hieght.

chief   might   height

4. My neice received the gift that I sent.

niece   received

Handwriting   Pp

Copy these sentences.
Practice making your p's correctly.

Peacocks parade in purple plumes.

Pink peony poses for a portrait.

Tuesday   Week 5   (61)

Page 62

Language Lines
Underline the possessive words in these sentences.
Add apostrophes where they are needed to show ownership.

1. The sun's rays melted the ice cream.
2. The students' portfolios were stored in the file.
3. The dogs' leashes broke as they chased the cat across the field.
4. The girl's skateboard was left on the playground.

Write a sentence with a possessive that uses 's.

Sentences will vary, but should use a singular possessive noun.

Write a sentence with a possessive that uses s'.

Sentences will vary, but should use a plural possessive noun.

MATH TIME
Continue the patterns.

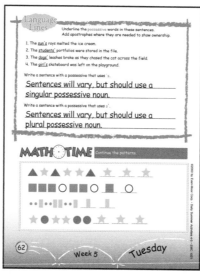

(62)   Week 5   Tuesday

Page 63

The Science Project

Just before the bell rang, Mr. Nielsen said, "Don't forget that your science projects are due a week from today."

Jose thought about his project. A few days ago he had found frog eggs at the pond near his house. He had scooped up a dozen or so eggs and some pond water in an empty jar. At home he placed the jar on top of the refrigerator to stay warm. The eggs looked like small black beads in white jelly.

Each day Jose looked at the eggs through a magnifying glass and drew what he saw. Day by day, he watched the jelly part of the eggs get smaller as the tadpoles grew in the black centers. Soon he could see heads and tails, and the tadpoles began to move. His science book said that the jelly part was food for the growing tadpoles.

The next Thursday the first of the eggs hatched. A tiny tadpole stuck itself to a leaf of the pond plant Jose had put in the jar. It had no mouth yet, but Jose could see fingerlike gills behind its head.

By Friday four more eggs had hatched. Jose carefully carried the jar to school, along with his day-by-day drawings and his journal of the changes he'd seen.

"This is a fine project, Jose," said Mr. Nielsen. "You must have given it a lot of thought."

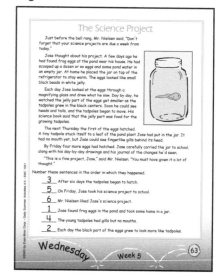

Number these sentences in the order in which they happened.

3   After six days the tadpoles began to hatch.
5   On Friday, Jose took his science project to school.
6   Mr. Nielsen liked Jose's science project.
1   Jose found frog eggs in the pond and took some home in a jar.
4   The young tadpoles had gills but no mouths.
2   Each day the black part of the eggs grew to look more like tadpoles.

Wednesday   Week 5   (63)

Page 64

Language Lines
Some possessives do not need apostrophes.
Circle the possessive form in each of these sentences.

1. The dog wagged its tail.
2. We spent our summer at camp.
3. My hat is on the table.
4. The roosters held their heads high.

Write a sentence that uses a possessive that does not need an apostrophe.

Sentences will vary.

MATH TIME
Find the answers.

1. Rafael can run one mile in 8.5 minutes. If he keeps up this speed, how long will it take him to run 5 miles?

42.5 minutes

2. Maria is selling T-shirts for her choir. Each shirt sells for $8. The choir keeps half of that as profit. If she sells 14 shirts, how much money will she have earned for the choir?

$56

3. Abby is half as old as her dad, but twice as old as her brother Sal. If Sal is 11, how old is their dad?

44 years old

(64)   Week 5   Wednesday

Page 65

Geography
Find what is located at these points.

Australia

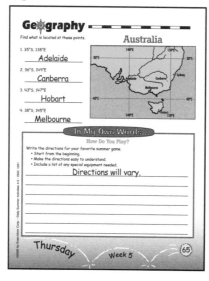

1. 35°S, 138°E
Adelaide

2. 36°S, 149°E
Canberra

3. 43°S, 147°E
Hobart

4. 38°S, 145°E
Melbourne

In My Own Words...
How Do You Play?

Write the directions for your favorite summer game.
• Start from the beginning.
• Make the directions easy to understand.
• Include a list of any special equipment needed.

Directions will vary.

Thursday   Week 5   (65)

Page 66

Language Lines
A comma is used to separate two or more adjectives listed together, unless one of the adjectives tells how many or is a color.
Add commas to the sentences below.

1. The little brown hen laid a round, spotted egg.
2. Sami had bright, curly ribbons in her long black hair.
3. Busy red ants scurried up the steep, slippery sides of their hill.
4. Would you like three tall boys to help you carry the heavy, bulging grocery bags?

Write a sentence about a girl and her dogs, using adjectives to describe how many and what kind.

Sentences will vary.

MATH TIME
Draw a picture to go with each problem. Draw the wholes and shade the parts represented by the two fractions. Then write the answer.

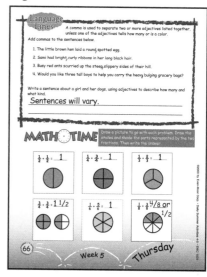

$\frac{1}{2} + \frac{1}{2} = 1$

$\frac{1}{4} + \frac{3}{4} = 1$

$\frac{1}{3} + \frac{2}{3} = 1$

$\frac{3}{4} + \frac{3}{4} = 1\frac{1}{2}$

$\frac{1}{8} + \frac{7}{8} = 1$

$\frac{1}{8} + \frac{3}{8} = \frac{4}{8}$ or $\frac{1}{2}$

(66)   Week 5   Thursday

Page 67

Language Lines
Use this with singular nouns. Use these with plural nouns.

Complete each sentence using this or these.

1. This slice of cake is yummy.
2. Will you help me put these chairs away?
3. This is the steepest hill in the neighborhood.
4. I want to put these books in my backpack.

Write a sentence using this as an adjective.

Sentences will vary.

Write a sentence using these as an adjective.

Sentences will vary.

MATH TIME
The median is the middle.

Write the median of each set of numbers.

	median
4, 7, 9, 10, 12, 14, 16	10
1, 3, 5, 7, 9, 11, 13	7
5, 10, 15, 20, 25	15
30, 31, 32, 33, 34, 35, 36	33

Friday   Week 5   (67)

Page 68

Syllogisms

Long ago in Greece, a famous thinker named Aristotle invented syllogisms. A syllogism has three sections. Facts are given in the first two sections. The third section is a new idea taken from the facts in the first two sections.

Example: All birds have feathers.
Chickens are birds.
Therefore, chickens have feathers.

A syllogism can be valid, without being true.

Example: All babies are cute.
No cute things cry.
Therefore, no babies cry.

Write the third line for each of the following syllogisms. Mark whether you think the syllogism is true or false.

All children like bubble gum.
All girls are children.
Therefore, all girls like bubble gum.   True (False)

All cats are purring animals.
All lions are cats.
Therefore, all lions purr.   True (False)

All stars are in the sky.
The sun is a star.
Therefore, the sun is in the sky.   (True) False

All apples grow on trees.
Granny Smiths are apples.
Therefore, Granny Smiths grow on trees.   (True) False

(68)   Week 5   Friday

Page 71

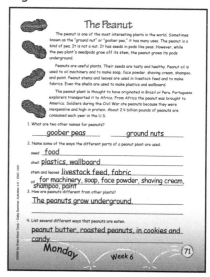

The Peanut

The peanut is one of the most interesting plants in the world. Sometimes known as the "ground nut" or "goober pea," it has many uses. The peanut is a kind of pea. It is not a nut. It has seeds in pods like peas. However, while the pea plant's seedpods grow off its stem, the peanut grows its pods underground.

Peanuts are useful plants. Their seeds are tasty and healthy. Peanut oil is used to oil machinery and to make soap, face powder, shaving cream, shampoo, and paint. Peanut stems and leaves are used in livestock feed and to make fabrics. Even the shells are used to make plastics and wallboard.

The peanut is thought to have originated in Brazil or Peru. Portuguese explorers transported it to Africa. From Africa the peanut was brought to America. Soldiers during the Civil War ate peanuts because they were inexpensive and high in protein. About 2.4 billion pounds of peanuts are consumed each year in the U.S.

1. What are two other names for peanuts?
goober peas   ground nuts

2. Name some of the ways the different parts of a peanut plant are used.
seed   food
shell   plastics, wallboard
stem and leaves   livestock feed, fabric
oil   for machinery, soap, face powder, shaving cream, shampoo, paint

3. How are peanuts different from other plants?
The peanuts grow underground.

4. List several different ways that peanuts are eaten.
peanut butter, roasted peanuts, in cookies and candy

Monday   Week 6   (71)

134

Page 72

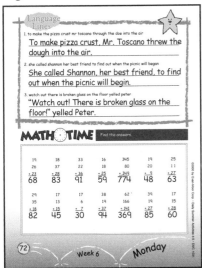

Language Lines

To make pizza crust mr toscano through the doe into the air

To make pizza crust, Mr. Toscano threw the dough into the air.

2. she called shannon her best friend to find out when the picnic will began

She called Shannon, her best friend, to find out when the picnic will begin.

3. watch out there is broken glass on the floor yelled peter

"Watch out! There is broken glass on the floor!" yelled Peter.

MATH TIME — Find the answers.

19	18	33	16	345	19	25
26	37	22	18	80	20	11
+ 23	+ 28	+ 36	+ 25	+ 349	+ 9	+ 27
68	83	91	59	774	48	63

29	17	17	38	62	39	17
35	13	6	19	166	19	15
+ 18	+ 15	+ 7	+ 37	+ 141	+ 27	+ 28
82	45	30	94	369	85	60

72   Week 6   Monday

Page 73

Spell It! Write the two words that make up each of these compound words. Draw a line to divide each word into syllables. Then write the number of syllables in each compound word.

without	with	out	2
myself	my	self	2
anybody	any	body	4
butterfly	butter	fly	3
basketball	basket	ball	3
homework	home	work	2
something	some	thing	2
secondhand	second	hand	3

Handwriting Copy these lines from the famous poem *Sea Fever* by John Masefield. Use your best handwriting.

I must go down to the seas again, to the lonely sea and the sky. And all I ask is a tall ship and a star to steer her by

Tuesday   Week 6   73

Page 74

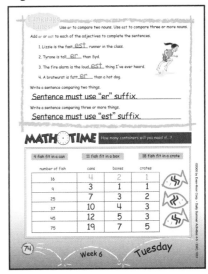

Language Lines — Use er to compare two nouns. Use est to compare three or more nouns.

Add er or est to each of the adjectives to complete the sentences.

1. Lizzie is the fast**est** runner in the class.

2. Tyrone is tall**er** than Syd.

3. The fire alarm is the loud**est** thing I've ever heard.

4. A bratwurst is fatt**er** than a hot dog.

Write a sentence comparing two things.

Sentence must use "er" suffix.

Write a sentence comparing three or more things.

Sentence must use "est" suffix.

MATH TIME — How many containers will you need if...?

	4 fish fit in a can	11 fish fit in a box	18 fish fit in a crate
number of fish	**cans**	**boxes**	**crates**
16	4	2	1
9	3	1	1
25	7	3	2
37	10	4	3
45	12	5	3
75	19	7	5

74   Week 6   Tuesday

Page 75

George Washington Carver
1864–1943

George Washington Carver grew up as a slave on a plantation in Missouri. As a boy, George loved plants! By the time he was seven, people in Diamond Grove, Missouri, called him "The Plant Doctor."

George was a skinny child with a high voice. He stuttered when he talked, but he was determined to learn as much as he could. When he was ten, he left home to find a town that would allow black children to go to school. He traveled through Missouri and Kansas, going to schools that would accept black students, until he graduated from high school. He opened his own laundry to pay his expenses.

In 1890 George began college. He studied art and then agriculture. He was the first black graduate of Iowa State College. Thomas Edison asked George to come to work in his laboratory, but George turned him down. George said that he wanted to help his people. So he set up an agricultural department at Tuskegee Normal School, a new university for black students in Alabama.

George Washington Carver became known as the "Wizard of Tuskegee." His work was instrumental in improving farming in the South. He is especially remembered for his peanut research. He discovered how to make 300 different things from the peanut plant.

1. What words would you use to describe George Washington Carver?

determined, hardworking, smart, helpful, etc.

2. What makes Dr. Carver's story so inspirational? He began life as a slave and through determination became an important scientist.

3. In this word search, find some of the products that Dr. Carver made from peanuts.

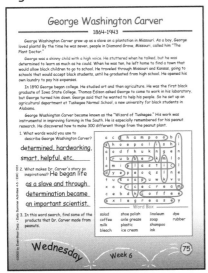

Word Box

salad   shoe polish   linoleum   dye
coffee   axle grease   soap   rubber
milk   plastic   shampoo
bleach   ice cream   ink

Wednesday   Week 6   75

Page 76

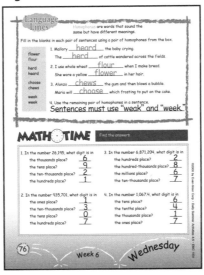

Language Lines — **Homophones** are words that sound the same but have different meanings.

Fill in the blanks in each pair of sentences using a pair of homophones from the box.

flower / flour
herd / heard
choose / chews
weak / week

1. Mallory **heard** the baby crying.
The **herd** of cattle wandered across the fields.

2. I use whole wheat **flour** when I make bread.
She wore a yellow **flower** in her hair.

3. Alonzo **chews** the gum and then blows a bubble.
Maria will **choose** which frosting to put on the cake.

4. Use the remaining pair of homophones in a sentence.

Sentences must use "weak" and "week."

MATH TIME — Find the answers.

1. In the number 26,195, what digit is in
the thousands place? **6**
the tens place? **9**
the ten-thousands place? **2**
the hundreds place? **1**

2. In the number 935,701, what digit is in
the ones place? **1**
the ten-thousands place? **3**
the tens place? **0**
the hundreds place? **7**

3. In the number 6,871,204, what digit is in
the hundreds place? **2**
the hundred-thousands place? **8**
the millions place? **6**
the ten-thousands place? **7**

4. In the number 1,067.4, what digit is in
the tens place? **6**
the tenths place? **4**
the thousands place? **1**
the ones place? **7**

76   Week 6   Wednesday

Page 77

Geography
Australia

This graph shows the population of the states and territories of Australia. Use the information to fill in the blanks and answer the question.

Western Australia   **1.9 million**
South Australia   **1.5 million**
Queensland   **3.4 million***
Northern Territory   **.2 million***
New South Wales   **6.2 million***
Victoria   **4.5 million**
Australian Capital Territory   **.4 million***
Tasmania   **.5 million**

How does the population of Victoria compare with the population of South Australia?

Victoria has about 3 million more people than South Australia.

* may vary slightly

In My Own Words... — *Summer Is Here!*

Write a chant or a cheer for summer. Practice reading it aloud. You may even want to make up actions to go with your words.

Chants will vary.

Example:
Sunny day, sunny day.
Bright bold, squinty ray.
Sunny day, sunny day.
Let's go out and play.

Thursday   Week 6   77

Page 78

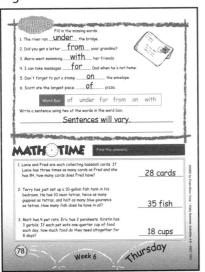

Language Lines — Fill in the missing words.

1. The river ran **under** the bridge.
2. Did you get a letter **from** your grandma?
3. Maria went swimming **with** her friends.
4. I can take messages **for** Dad when he's not home.
5. Don't forget to put a stamp **on** the envelope.
6. Scott ate the largest piece **of** pizza.

Word Box of under for from on with

Write a sentence using two of the words in the word box.

Sentences will vary.

MATH TIME — Find the answers.

1. Lanie and Fred are each collecting baseball cards. If Lanie has three times as many cards as Fred and she has 84, how many cards does Fred have?   **28 cards**

2. Terry has just set up a 10-gallon fish tank in his bedroom. He has 10 neon tetras, twice as many guppies as tetras, and half as many blue gouramis as tetras. How much fish does he have in all?   **35 fish**

3. Matt has 4 pet rats. Eric has 2 parakeets. Kirstin has 4 gerbils. If each pet eats one-quarter cup of food each day, how much pet food do they need altogether for 8 days?   **18 cups**

78   Week 6   Thursday

Page 79

Language Lines — Write contractions to complete the sentences.

I'm (I am) going to the park to play. My friend Thomas **can't** (can not) come with me. His mother **isn't** (is not) feeling well, so he will stay home. After **I've** (I have) finished playing, **I'll** (I will) go to the library and check out a book. Then **I'll** (I will) take the book over to Thomas so he **won't** (will not) feel lonely.

MATH TIME — Solve the problems. Then use the key to answer the riddles.

What has eyes but cannot see? **P O T A T O**

662	504	734	426	845	615
− 275	− 166	− 157	− 379	− 268	− 277
387	338	577	47	577	338

What has ears but cannot hear? **C O R N**

356	723	783	912
− 278	− 385	− 388	− 667
78	338	395	245

What has a tongue but cannot talk? **S H O E**

614	524	836	347
− 187	− 237	− 498	− 168
427	287	179	

Key   47 = a   227 = h   395 = r   78 = c   245 = n
179 = e   338 = o   577 = t   387 = p   427 = s

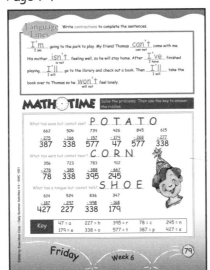

Friday   Week 6   79

Page 80

Read this recipe for making peanut butter candy.
Follow the directions and ask an adult to help.

MMMmmm...

Candy Marbles!!

What You Need
½ cup of chunky peanut butter
½ cup of evaporated milk
½ cup of brown sugar
1 teaspoon of cinnamon
1 cup of crispy chow mein noodles, slightly crushed
1 cup of stick pretzels, slightly crushed
1 cup of chopped nuts

What You Do
1. Stir the peanut butter, evaporated milk, brown sugar, and cinnamon together in a saucepan.
2. Cook over medium heat for five minutes.
3. Remove from heat. Stir in noodles, pretzels, and nuts.
4. Drop spoonfuls onto a foil-lined cookie sheet.
5. Chill for one hour.
6. Pop one in your mouth for a yummy treat!

80   Week 6   Friday

Page 83

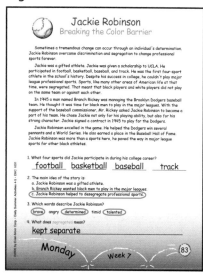

Jackie Robinson
Breaking the Color Barrier

Sometimes a tremendous change can occur through an individual's determination. Jackie Robinson overcame discrimination and segregation to change professional sports forever.

Jackie was a gifted athlete. Jackie was given a scholarship to UCLA. He participated in football, basketball, baseball, and track. He was the first four-sport athlete in the school's history. Despite his success in college, he couldn't play major league professional sports. Sports, like many other areas of American life at that time, were segregated. That meant that black players and white players did not play on the same team or against each other.

In 1945 a man named Branch Rickey was managing the Brooklyn Dodgers baseball team. He thought it was time for black men to play in the major leagues. With the support of the baseball commissioner, Mr. Rickey asked Jackie Robinson to become a part of his team. He chose Jackie not only for his playing ability, but also for his strong character. Jackie signed a contract in 1945 to play for the Dodgers.

Jackie Robinson excelled in the game. He helped the Dodgers win several pennants and a World Series. He also earned a place in the Baseball Hall of Fame. Jackie Robinson was more than a sports hero, he paved the way in major league sports for other black athletes.

1. What four sports did Jackie participate in during his college career?
   football   basketball   baseball   track

2. The main idea of the story is:
   a. Jackie Robinson was a gifted athlete.
   b. Branch Rickey wanted black men to play in the major leagues.
   c. Jackie Robinson helped to desegregate professional sports.

3. Which words describe Jackie Robinson?
   brave   angry   determined   timid   talented

4. What does *segregated* mean?
   kept separate

Monday   Week 7   83

Page 84

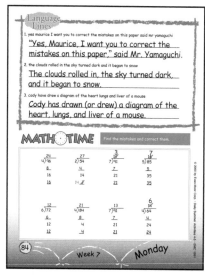

Language Lines

1. yes maurice I want you to correct the mistakes on this paper said mr yamoguchi
   "Yes, Maurice, I want you to correct the mistakes on this paper," said Mr. Yamaguchi.

2. the clouds rolled in the sky turned dark and it began to snow
   The clouds rolled in, the sky turned dark, and it began to snow.

3. cody have drew a diagram of the heart lungs and liver of a mouse
   Cody has drawn (or drew) a diagram of the heart, lungs, and liver of a mouse.

MATH TIME — Find the mistakes and correct them.

```
    24              27            3           7
4)96            2)54          7)91        5)85
                                          ³⁵
  8               4             6           35
  16              14            21          35
  16              14 X          21          35

   12              21           13           6
6)72            4)84         7)91        4)64
  6               8            7            4
  12              4            21           24
  12              4            21           24
```

84   Week 7   Monday

Page 85

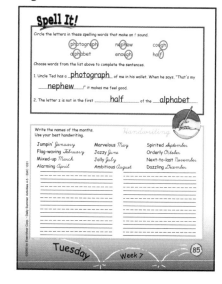

Spell It!

Circle the letters in these spelling words that make an *f* sound.

photograph   nephew   cough
alphabet   enough   half

Choose words from the list above to complete the sentences.

1. Uncle Ted has a **photograph** of me in his wallet. When he says, "That's my **nephew**," it makes me feel good.

2. The letter z is not in the first **half** of the **alphabet**.

Handwriting

Write the names of the months.
Use your best handwriting.

Jumpin' *January*   Marvelous *May*   Spirited *September*
Flag-waving *February*   Jazzy *June*   Orderly *October*
Mixed-up *March*   Jolly *July*   Next-to-last *November*
Alarming *April*   Ambitious *August*   Dazzling *December*

Tuesday   Week 7   85

Page 86

Language Lines   Write the correct abbreviation for each word.

Avenue	Ave.	Street	St.
Mister	Mr.	tablespoon	tbsp.
foot	ft.	Junior	Jr.
pound	lb.	quart	qt.
Doctor	Dr.	centimeter	cm

qt.   Ave.   lb.   Jr.   St.
tbsp.   cm   Mr.   Dr.   ft.

MATH TIME — Find the answers.

1. Maurice is three times as tall as his brother. If Maurice is 5 feet, 3 inches tall, how tall is his brother? (Hint: Change Maurice's height to inches.)   **21 inches**

2. Betty has 15 beanbag animals. If she gives ⅓ of them to her sister, how many will she have left?   **10 animals**

3. Murphy is walking dogs to earn some spending money. If he gets paid $2.50 per dog and he needs $18.00, how many dogs must he walk?   **8 dogs**

86   Week 7   Tuesday

Page 87

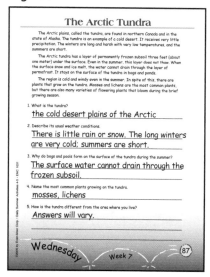

The Arctic Tundra

The Arctic plains, called the tundra, are found in northern *Canada* and in the state of Alaska. The tundra is an example of a cold desert. It receives very little precipitation. The winters are long and harsh with very low temperatures, and the summers are short.

The Arctic tundra has a layer of permanently frozen subsoil three feet (about one meter) under the surface. Even in the summer, this layer does not thaw. When the surface snow and ice melt, the water cannot drain through the layer of permafrost. It stays on the surface of the tundra in bogs and ponds.

The region is cold and windy even in the summer. In spite of this, there are plants that grow on the tundra. Mosses and lichens are the most common plants, but there are also many varieties of flowering plants that bloom during the brief growing season.

1. What is the tundra?
   the cold desert plains of the Arctic

2. Describe its usual weather conditions.
   There is little rain or snow. The long winters are very cold; summers are short.

3. Why do bogs and pools form on the surface of the tundra during the summer?
   The surface water cannot drain through the frozen subsoil.

4. Name the most common plants growing on the tundra.
   mosses, lichens

5. How is the tundra different from the area where you live?
   Answers will vary.

Wednesday   Week 7   87

Page 88

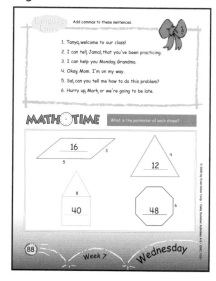

Language Lines   Add commas to these sentences.

1. Tanya, welcome to our class!
2. I can tell, Jamal, that you've been practicing.
3. I can help you Monday, Grandma.
4. Okay Mom, I'm on my way.
5. Sal, can you tell me how to do this problem?
6. Hurry up, Mark, or we're going to be late.

MATH TIME — What is the perimeter of each shape?

16 (parallelogram)   12 (triangle)
40 (pentagon)   48 (octagon)

88   Week 7   Wednesday

Page 89

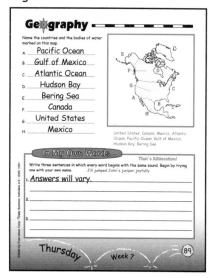

Geography

Name the countries and the bodies of water marked on this map.

A. Pacific Ocean
B. Gulf of Mexico
C. Atlantic Ocean
D. Hudson Bay
E. Bering Sea
F. Canada
G. United States
H. Mexico

United States, Canada, Mexico, Atlantic Ocean, Pacific Ocean, Gulf of Mexico, Hudson Bay, Bering Sea

In My Own Words...
That's Alliteration!

Write three sentences in which every word begins with the same sound. Begin by trying one with your own name.   Jill jumped John's juniper joyfully.

1. Answers will vary.
2.
3.

Thursday   Week 7   89

Page 90

Language Lines   Add commas to this letter.

410 Park Street
Funville, Ohio
July 30, 2000

Dear Pete,

Thank you for the super new shirt. I like the logo, the color, and the material. You sure know how to pick out a good present! I hope that you can come to visit soon. We can go to the zoo, have a picnic, and see a movie.
Thanks again.

Your pal,
Fred

MATH TIME — Find the answers.

```
 2317     4139     5216     5349     3725     3148
+1425    -2524    +1208    -2616    +5215    -2607
 3742     1615     6424     2733     8940      541

 3522     6417     7346     1509     5537     2424
+4138    -2514    +2129    -1274    +4127    -1028
 7660     3903     9475      235     9664     1396
```

90   Week 7   Thursday

Page 91

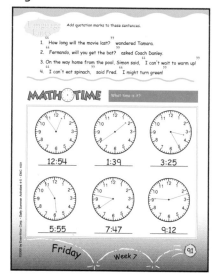

Language Lines   Add quotation marks to these sentences.

1. How long will the movie last? wondered Tamara.
2. Fernando, will you get the bat? asked Coach Danley.
3. On the way home from the pool, Simon said, I can't wait to warm up!
4. I can't eat spinach, said Fred. I might turn green!

MATH TIME — What time is it?

12:54   1:39   3:25
5:55   7:47   9:12

Friday   Week 7   91

Page 92

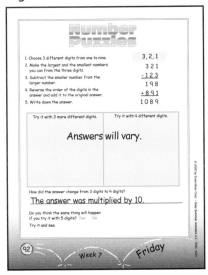

Number Puzzles

1. Choose 3 different digits from one to nine. 3, 2, 1
2. Make the largest and the smallest numbers you can from the three digits. 321
3. Subtract the smaller number from the larger number. -123
   198
4. Reverse the order of the digits in the answer and add it to the original answer. +891
   1089
5. Write down the answer. 1089

Try it with 3 more different digits.	Try it with 4 different digits.
Answers will vary.	

How did the answer change from 3 digits to 4 digits?
The answer was multiplied by 10.

Do you think the same thing will happen if you try it with 5 digits? Yes No
Try it and see.

(92) Week 7 Friday

Page 95

Ordering from a Catalog

Fill in the order form below as if you were ordering the three items shown. Pretend that your shoe size is 8 and that you want a silver helmet.

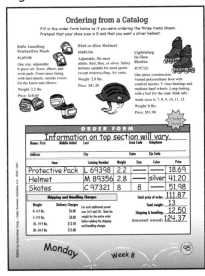

Safe Landing Protective Pack
#L69398
One size, adjustable 6-piece set. Knee, elbow, and wrist pads. Foam inner lining with hard plastic outside covers for the knees and elbows.
Weight: 2.2 lbs.
Price: $18.69

Dial-a-Size Helmet
#MI9356
Adjustable, fits most adults. Red, blue, or silver. Safety helmets suitable for most sports except motorcycling. Air vents.
Weight: 2.8 lbs.
Price: $41.20

Lightning In-line Skates
#C97321
One-piece construction. Vented polyurethane boot with comfort insoles. Y class bearings and medium-hard wheels. Long-lasting, with a feel for the road. Rink safe.
Adult sizes 6, 7, 8, 9, 10, 11, 12
Weight: 8 lbs.
Price: $51.98

ORDER FORM

Information on top section will vary.

Name: First Middle Initial Last Area Code Telephone
Address City State Zip Code

Item	Catalog Number	Weight	Size	Color	Price
Protective Pack	L 69398	2.2			18.69
Helmet	M 89356	2.8		silver	41.20
Skates	C 97321	8	8		51.98
				Total price of order:	111.87

Shipping and Handling Charges			
Weight	Delivery Charges	Total weight:	13
0–4.9 lbs.	$6.00	Shipping & handling:	12.50
5–9.9 lbs.	$8.00	Amount owed:	124.37
10–19.9 lbs.	$12.50		
20–34.9 lbs.	$15.00		

For each additional pound over 34.9 add 25¢. Total the weight for the entire order before adding the shipping and handling charges.

Monday Week 8 (95)

Page 96

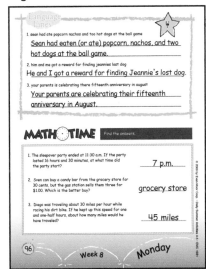

Language Lines

1. sean had ate popcorn nachos and too hot dogs at the ball game
   Sean had eaten (or ate) popcorn, nachos, and two hot dogs at the ball game.

2. him and me got a reward for finding jeannies lost dog
   He and I got a reward for finding Jeannie's lost dog.

3. your parents are celebrating there fifteenth anniversary in august
   Your parents are celebrating their fifteenth anniversary in August.

MATH TIME Find the answers.

1. The sleepover party ended at 11:30 a.m. If the party lasted 16 hours and 30 minutes, at what time did the party start? **7 p.m.**

2. Sven can buy a candy bar from the grocery store for 30 cents, but the gas station sells them three for $1.00. Which is the better buy? **grocery store**

3. Diego was traveling about 30 miles per hour while racing his dirt bike. If he kept up this speed for one and one-half hours, about how many miles would he have traveled? **45 miles**

(96) Week 8 Monday

Page 97

Spell It! Fill in the missing letters.

oi oy		u e ew ue	
v_oi_ce	t_oy_al	tr_u_th	n_ew_s
v_oy_age	disapp_oi_nt	d_ue_	_u_sed
n_oi_se	destr_oy_	men_u_	f_u_ture

Write these ice-cream flavors. *Handwriting*

rocky road and vanilla
strawberry and bubble gum
butter pecan and chocolate
cookies 'n cream and lemon sour

_____
_____
_____
_____

What's your favorite flavor? Why?
Answers will vary.

Tuesday Week 8 (97)

Page 98

Language Lines

Copy these sentences. Use capital letters where they are needed.

1. my friend joyce lives in evanston illinois
   My friend Joyce lives in Evanston, Illinois.

2. dr cook said that i could get my cast off on august 4
   Dr. Cook said that I could get my cast off on August 4.

3. jo said that jungle book was her favorite movie
   Jo said that Jungle Book was her favorite movie.

MATH TIME Find the answers.

51	67	38	24	45	26	75	96
x65	x54	x72	x36	x36	x58	x92	x29
3315	3618	2736	2232	1620	1508	6900	2784

74	93	48	13	71	86	59	27
x86	x24	x75	x83	x20	x46	x38	x69
6364	2232	3600	1079	1420	3956	2242	1863

(98) Week 8 Tuesday

Page 99

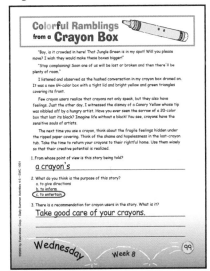

Colorful Ramblings from a Crayon Box

"Boy, is it crowded in here! That Jungle Green is in my spot! Will you please move? I wish they would make these boxes bigger!"

"Stop complaining! Soon one of us will be lost or broken and then there'll be plenty of room."

I listened and observed as the hushed conversation in my crayon box droned on. It was a new 64-color box with a tight lid and bright yellow and green triangles covering its front.

Few crayon users realize that crayons not only speak, but they also have feelings. Just the other day, I witnessed the dismay of a Canary Yellow whose tip was nibbled off by a hungry artist. Have you ever seen the sorrow of a 20-color box that lost its black? Imagine life without a black! You see, crayons have the sensitive souls of artists.

The next time you use a crayon, think about the fragile feelings hidden under the ripped paper covering. Think of the shame and hopelessness in the lost-crayon tub. Take the time to return your crayons to their rightful home. Use them wisely so that their creative potential is realized.

1. From whose point of view is this story being told?
   a crayon's

2. What do you think is the purpose of this story?
   a. to give directions
   b. to inform
   c. to entertain

3. There is a recommendation for crayon users in the story. What is it?
   Take good care of your crayons.

Wednesday Week 8 (99)

Page 100

Language Lines

Use I or me in each sentence.

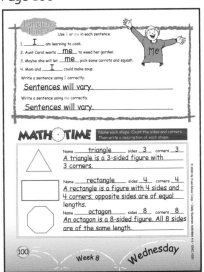

1. _I_ am learning to cook.
2. Aunt Carol wants _me_ to weed her garden.
3. Maybe she will let _me_ pick some carrots and squash.
4. Mom and _I_ could make soup.

Write a sentence using I correctly.
Sentences will vary.

Write a sentence using me correctly.
Sentences will vary.

MATH TIME Name each shape. Count the sides and corners. Then write a description of each shape.

Name _triangle_ sides _3_ corners _3_
A triangle is a 3-sided figure with 3 corners.

Name _rectangle_ sides _4_ corners _4_
A rectangle is a figure with 4 sides and 4 corners; opposite sides are of equal lengths.

Name _octagon_ sides _8_ corners _8_
An octagon is a 8-sided figure. All 8 sides are of the same length.

(100) Week 8 Wednesday

Page 101

Geography

Locate each body of water on this map. Write its letter.

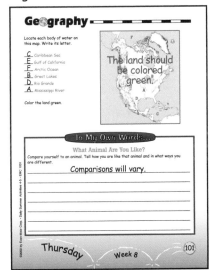

The land should be colored green.

_C_ Caribbean Sea
_F_ Gulf of California
_E_ Arctic Ocean
_B_ Great Lakes
_D_ Rio Grande
_A_ Mississippi River

Color the land green.

In My Own Words…
What Animal Are You Like?

Compare yourself to an animal. Tell how you are like that animal and in what ways you are different.

Comparisons will vary.

_____
_____
_____

Thursday Week 8 (101)

Page 102

Language Lines Circle the correct words.

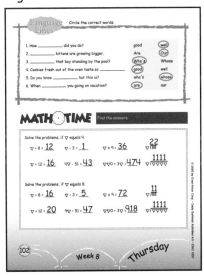

1. How _____ did you do? good **well**
2. _____ kittens are growing bigger. Are **Our**
3. _____ that boy standing by the pool? **Who's** Whose
4. Cookies fresh out of the oven taste so _____. good **well**
5. Do you know _____ hat this is? who's **whose**
6. When _____ you going on vacation? **are** our

MATH TIME Find the answers.

Solve the problems, if ▽ equals 4.

▽ ÷ 8 = **12**   ▽ – 3 = **1**   ▽ × 9 = **36**   ▽⁄₈₈ **22**/₈₈

▽ ÷ 12 = **16**   9▽ – 51 = **43**   ▽▽0 ÷ 3▽ = **474**   ▽⁄▽▽▽▽ **1111**/▽▽▽▽

Solve the problems, if ▽ equals 8.

▽ ÷ 8 = **16**   ▽ – 3 = **5**   ▽ × 9 = **72**   ▽⁄₈₈ **11**/₈₈

▽ ÷ 12 = **20**   9▽ – 51 = **47**   ▽▽0 ÷ 3▽ = **918**   ▽⁄▽▽▽▽ **1111**/▽▽▽▽

(102) Week 8 Thursday

137

©2005 by Evan-Moor Corp. • Daily Summer Activities 4–5 • EMC 1031

Page 103

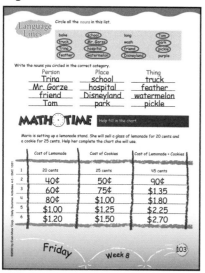

Circle all the nouns in this list.

bake · **school** · long · **Tom**
Truck · **Mr. Gorze** · wash · **bank**
Trina · **hospital** · **friend** · **pickle**
feather · **watermelon** · **Disneyland** · purple

Write the nouns you circled in the correct category.

Person	Place	Thing
Trina	school	truck
Mr. Gorze	hospital	feather
friend	Disneyland	watermelon
Tom	park	pickle

MATH TIME Help fill in the chart.

Maria is setting up a lemonade stand. She will sell a glass of lemonade for 20 cents and a cookie for 25 cents. Help her complete the chart she will use.

	Cost of Lemonade	Cost of Cookies	Cost of Lemonade + Cookies
1	20 cents	25 cents	45 cents
2	40¢	50¢	90¢
3	60¢	75¢	$1.35
4	80¢	$1.00	$1.80
5	$1.00	$1.25	$2.25
6	$1.20	$1.50	$2.70

Friday Week 8 103

Page 104

What Is It?

Plot these coordinate pairs on the grid. Then connect the points to make a picture.

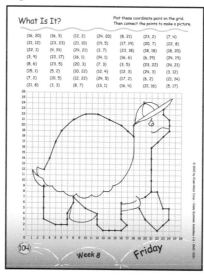

(16, 20) (16, 3) (12, 2) (24, 20) (8, 21) (23, 2) (7, 4)
(21, 12) (23, 23) (21, 10) (19, 5) (17, 19) (20, 7) (22, 8)
(22, 1) (4, 14) (24, 21) (3, 7) (23, 18) (18, 20) (18, 20)
(3, 9) (22, 17) (16, 1) (14, 1) (16, 6) (6, 19) (24, 19)
(8, 6) (23, 5) (20, 3) (7, 3) (3, 5) (23, 2) (14, 21)
(15, 1) (5, 2) (10, 22) (12, 4) (12, 3) (24, 3) (3, 12)
(7, 2) (10, 5) (22, 22) (24, 5) (6, 2) (21, 14)
(21, 8) (3, 3) (8, 7) (13, 1) (16, 4) (21, 16) (5, 17)

104 Week 8 Friday

Page 107

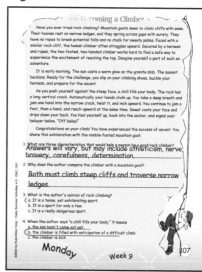

On Becoming a Climber

Have you ever tried rock climbing? Mountain goats seem to climb cliffs with ease. Their hooves rest on narrow ledges, and they spring across gaps with surety. They have no ropes to break potential falls and no chalk for sweaty palms. Faced with a similar rock cliff, the human climber often struggles upward. Secured by a harness and ropes, the two-footed, two-handed climber works hard to find a safe way to experience the excitement of reaching the top. Imagine yourself a part of such an adventure.

It is early morning. The sun casts a warm glow on the granite slab. The summit beckons. Ready for the challenge, you slip on your climbing shoes, buckle your harness, and prepare for the ascent.

As you push yourself against the steep face, a chill fills your body. The rock has a long vertical crack. Automatically your hands chalk up. You take a deep breath and jam one hand into the narrow crack, twist it, and inch upward. You continue to jam a foot, then a hand, and reach upward at the same time. Sweat coats your face and drips down your back. You haul yourself up, hook into the anchor, and signal your belayer below, "Off belay!"

Congratulations on your climb! You have experienced the success of ascent. You share this exhilaration with the nimble-footed mountain goat.

1. What are three characteristics that would help a person be a good rock climber?
Answers will vary, but may include athleticism, nerve, bravery, carefulness, determination.

2. Why does the author compare the climber with a mountain goat?
Both must climb steep cliffs and traverse narrow ledges.

3. What is the author's opinion of rock climbing?
   a. It is a tense, yet exhilarating sport.
   b. It is a sport for only a few.
   c. It is a really dangerous sport.

4. When the author says "a chill fills your body," it means
   a. the sun hasn't come out yet
   b. the climber is filled with anticipation of a difficult climb
   c. the climber is sick

Monday Week 9 107

Page 108

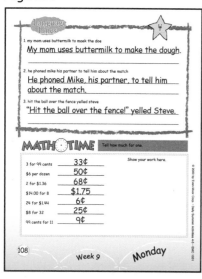

1. my mom uses buttermilk to maek the doe
My mom uses buttermilk to make the dough.

2. he phoned mike his partner to tell him about the match
He phoned Mike, his partner, to tell him about the match.

3. hit the ball over the fence yelled steve
"Hit the ball over the fence!" yelled Steve.

MATH TIME Tell how much for one.

		Show your work here.
3 for 99 cents	**33¢**	
$6 per dozen	**50¢**	
2 for $1.36	**68¢**	
$14.00 for 8	**$1.75**	
24 for $1.44	**6¢**	
$8 for 32	**25¢**	
99 cents for 11	**9¢**	

108 Week 9 Monday

Page 109

Spell It!

Circle the words that are spelled correctly.

1. althoa	althoue	**although**
2. **cousin**	cusin	coosin
3. shure	**sure**	sher
4. whitch	wich	**which**
5. minet	**minute**	minit
6. truble	trable	**trouble**

Handwriting

Copy this paragraph about owls.

Owls are nocturnal hunters. They catch and eat small rodents. In fact, a single barn owl can eat over one thousand mice in just one year.

Tuesday Week 9 109

Page 110

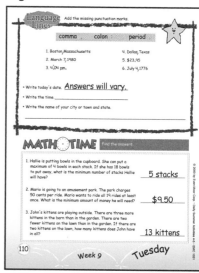

Add the missing punctuation marks.

comma   colon   period

1. Boston, Massachusetts
2. March 7, 1980
3. 4:04 pm,
4. Dallas, Texas
5. $23.95
6. July 4, 1776

• Write today's date. **Answers will vary.**
• Write the time.
• Write the name of your city or town and state.

MATH TIME Find the answer.

1. Hallie is putting bowls in the cupboard. She can put a maximum of 4 bowls in each stack. If she has 18 bowls to put away, what is the minimum number of stacks Hallie will have?   **5 stacks**

2. Mario is going to an amusement park. The park charges 50 cents per ride. Mario wants to ride all 19 rides at least once. What is the minimum amount of money he will need?   **$9.50**

3. John's kittens are playing outside. There are three more kittens in the barn than in the garden. There are two fewer kittens on the lawn than in the garden. If there are two kittens on the lawn, how many kittens does John have in all?   **13 kittens**

110 Week 9 Tuesday

Page 111

How Stories Began...

One cold winter day, a boy went hunting. After he had shot several partridges, he sat down beside a great rock to rest. A deep voice came from the rock. "Listen, I will tell you a story." The boy jumped to his feet. There was no one around.

He called out, "Who are you? What is a story?"

"I am the Great Stone. I have been here since the beginning of time. I can tell you how things came to be," the voice rumbled from the rock.

The boy trembled at the power of the voice. Could it be the stone talking to him? He stood his ground and said, "Great Stone, tell your story."

"First you must give me something," said the stone.

The boy took one of the partridges he had just killed and placed it on the rock. "Here is a bird for you, Great One. Now tell your story," said the boy, sitting back down.

The Great Stone began to speak. His words rumbled from the ground, telling a wonderful story of how the earth had been made. As the stone spoke, the boy listened. He didn't feel the cold wind or snow. He seemed warm inside. When the story was over, the boy stood to leave. "Thank you, Great One. I must go share your story with my family. I will be back tomorrow."

1. What startled the boy at the beginning of the story?
The rock spoke to him.

2. What exchange did the boy and the Great Stone make?
The boy gave the stone a partridge in exchange for the story.

3. Did you like the story? Tell why you think the way you do.
Responses will vary.

4. A partridge is
   a. a type of bird
   b. a small rabbit
   c. a wild deer

5. Rumbled means
   a. laughed cheerfully
   b. spoke in soft, quiet tones
   c. made a deep, rolling sound

Wednesday Week 9 111

Page 112

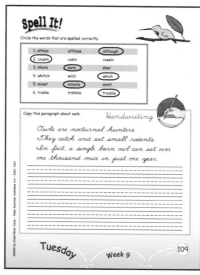

Use *we* or *us* in each sentence.

1. Can **we** make some cookies?
2. It is time for **us** to go to practice.
3. It was fun for **us** to sleep in the tent.
4. **We** have a new kitten.

Write a sentence using *we*.
Sentences will vary.

Write a sentence using *us*.
Sentences will vary.

MATH TIME Find the answers.

3(4) = **12**	7(8) = **56**	5(6) = **30**	9(2) = **18**	10(8) = **80**	72(2) = **144**
12(6) = **72**	10(10) = **100**	25(1) = **25**	4(9) = **36**	8(3) = **24**	51(3) = **153**
2(7) = **14**	6(5) = **30**	11(4) = **44**	12(12) = **144**	11(9) = **99**	36(0) = **0**

112 Week 9 Wednesday

Page 113

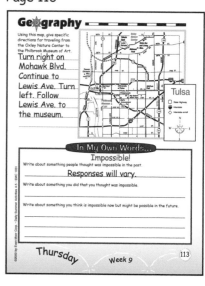

Geography

Using this map, give specific directions for traveling from the Oxley Nature Center to the Philbrook Museum of Art.
Turn right on Mohawk Blvd. Continue to Lewis Ave. Turn left. Follow Lewis Ave. to the museum.

Tulsa

In My Own Words...
Impossible!

Write about something people thought was impossible in the past.
Responses will vary.

Write about something you did that you thought was impossible.

Write about something you think is impossible now but might be possible in the future.

Thursday Week 9 113

Page 114

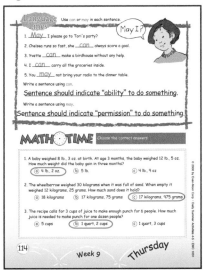

Language Lines — Use *can* or *may* in each sentence.

1. _May_ I please go to Toni's party?
2. Chelsea runs so fast, she _can_ always score a goal.
3. Yvette _can_ make a birdhouse without any help.
4. I _can_ carry all the groceries inside.
5. You _may_ not bring your radio to the dinner table.

May I?

Write a sentence using *can*.
Sentence should indicate "ability" to do something.

Write a sentence using *may*.
Sentence should indicate "permission" to do something.

MATH TIME — Choose the correct answers.

1. A baby weighed 8 lb., 3 oz. at birth. At age 3 months, the baby weighed 12 lb., 5 oz. How much weight did the baby gain in three months?
   (a) 4 lb., 2 oz.   (b) 5 lb.   (c) 4 lb., 9 oz.

2. The wheelbarrow weighed 30 kilograms when it was full of sand. When empty it weighed 12 kilograms, 25 grams. How much sand does it hold?
   (a) 18 kilograms   (b) 17 kilograms, 75 grams   (c) 17 kilograms, 975 grams

3. The recipe calls for 3 cups of juice to make enough punch for 6 people. How much juice is needed to make punch for one dozen people?
   (a) 5 cups   (b) 1 quart, 2 cups   (c) 1 quart, 3 cups

114 | Week 9 | Thursday

Page 115

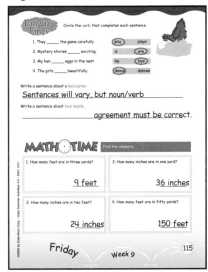

Language Lines — Circle the verb that completes each sentence.

1. They _____ the game carefully.   play / (plays)
2. Mystery stories _____ exciting.   is / (are)
3. My hen _____ eggs in the nest.   lay / (lays)
4. The girls _____ beautifully.   (dance) / dances

Write a sentence about *a helicopter*.
Sentences will vary, but noun/verb

Write a sentence about *four snails*.
_____ agreement must be correct.

MATH TIME — Find the answers.

1. How many feet are in three yards?
   9 feet

2. How many inches are in one yard?
   36 inches

3. How many inches are in two feet?
   24 inches

4. How many feet are in fifty yards?
   150 feet

Friday | Week 9 | 115

Page 116

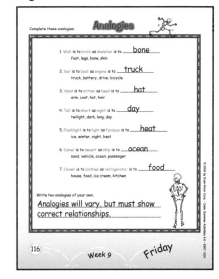

Complete these analogies.

Analogies

1. Wall is to brick as skeleton is to _bone_
   foot, legs, bone, skin

2. Sail is to boat as engine is to _truck_
   truck, battery, drive, bicycle

3. Hand is to mitten as head is to _hat_
   arm, coat, hat, hair

4. Tall is to short as night is to _day_
   twilight, dark, long, day

5. Flashlight is to light as furnace is to _heat_
   ice, winter, night, heat

6. Camel is to desert as ship is to _ocean_
   sand, vehicle, ocean, passenger

7. Closet is to clothes as refrigerator is to _food_
   house, food, ice cream, kitchen

Write two analogies of your own.
Analogies will vary, but must show
correct relationships.

116 | Week 9 | Friday

Page 119

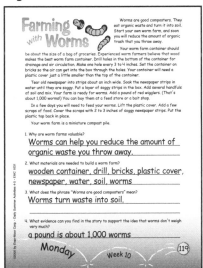

Farming with Worms

Worms are good composters. They eat organic waste and turn it into soil. Start your own worm farm, and soon you will reduce the amount of organic trash that you throw away.

be about the size of a bag of groceries. Experienced worm farmers believe that wood makes the best worm farm container. Drill holes in the bottom of the container for drainage and air circulation. Make one hole every 3 to 4 inches. Set the container on bricks so the air can get into the box through the holes. Your container will need a plastic cover just a little smaller than the top of the container.

Tear old newspaper into strips about an inch wide. Soak the newspaper strips in water until they are soggy. Put a layer of soggy strips in the box. Add several handfuls of soil and mix. Your farm is ready for worms. Add a pound of red wigglers. (That's about 1,000 worms!) You can buy them at a feed store or a bait shop.

In a few days you will need to feed your worms. Lift the plastic cover. Add a few scraps of food. Cover the scraps with 2 to 3 inches of soggy newspaper strips. Put the plastic top back in place.

Your worm farm is a miniature compost pile.

1. Why are worm farms valuable?
Worms can help you reduce the amount of organic waste you throw away.

2. What materials are needed to build a worm farm?
wooden container, drill, bricks, plastic cover, newspaper, water, soil, worms

3. What does the phrase "Worms are good composters" mean?
Worms turn waste into soil.

4. What evidence can you find in the story to support the idea that worms don't weigh very much?
a pound is about 1,000 worms

Monday | Week 10 | 119

Page 120

Language Lines ⭐

1. did you see the rattlesnake special on pbs i seen it twice
   Did you see the rattlesnake special on PBS? I saw it twice.

2. me and my family is visiting orlando florida for an week said dr luiz
   "My family and I are visiting Orlando, Florida, for a week," said Dr. Luiz.

3. the clown selected marco my oldest brother two be her helper
   The clown selected Marco, my oldest brother, to be her helper.

MATH TIME — Find the answers

1. During the soccer season, Rosa scored at least one point in half of her games. If she played 8 games, in how many games did Rosa score?
   4 games

2. Andy is baking muffins for breakfast. Each box makes 8 muffins. If he wants to make at least 30 muffins, how many boxes will he need to use?
   4 boxes

3. Kane's desk has three drawers in it. In each drawer he has 12 puzzles. How many puzzles does he have in all?
   36 puzzles

120 | Week 10 | Monday

Page 121

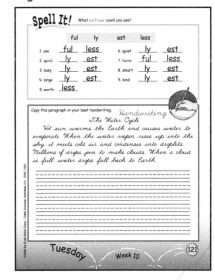

Spell It! — What suffixes could you use?

	ful	ly	est	less

1. use _ful_ _less_   6. quiet _ly_ _est_
2. quick _ly_ _est_   7. harm _ful_ _less_
3. busy _ly_ _est_   8. small _ly_ _est_
4. large _ly_ _est_   9. kind _ly_ _est_
5. worth _less_

Copy this paragraph in your best handwriting. — *Handwriting*

The Water Cycle
Hot sun warms the Earth and causes water to evaporate. When the water vapor rises up into the sky, it meets cold air and condenses into droplets. Millions of drops join to make clouds. When a cloud is full, water drops fall back to Earth.

Tuesday | Week 10 | 121

Page 122

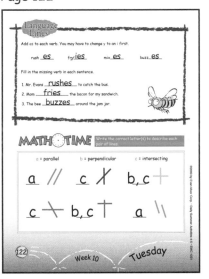

Language Lines

Add *es* to each verb. You may have to change *y* to *i* first.

rush _es_   fry _ies_   mix _es_   buzz _es_

Fill in the missing verb in each sentence.

1. Mr. Evans _rushes_ to catch the bus.
2. Mom _fries_ the bacon for my sandwich.
3. The bee _buzzes_ around the jam jar.

MATH TIME — Write the correct letter(s) to describe each pair of lines.

a = parallel   b = perpendicular   c = intersecting

a //   c X   b,c +

c +   b,c +   a ||

122 | Week 10 | Tuesday

Page 123

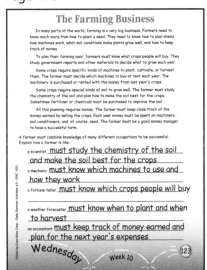

The Farming Business

In many parts of the world, farming is a very big business. Farmers need to know much more than how to plant a seed. They need to know how to plan ahead, how machines work, what soil conditions make plants grow well, and how to keep track of money.

To plan their farming year, farmers must know what crops people will buy. They study government reports and other materials to decide what to grow each year.

Some crops require specific kinds of machines to plant, cultivate, or harvest them. The farmer must decide which machines to buy or rent each year. The machinery is purchased or rented with the money from last year's crops.

Some crops require special kinds of soil to grow well. The farmer must study the chemistry of the soil and plan how to plant the soil best for the crops. Sometimes fertilizer or chemicals must be purchased to improve the soil.

All this planning requires money. The farmer must keep close track of the money earned by selling the crops. Each year money must be spent on machinery, soil conditioners, and, of course, seed. The farmer must be a good money manager to have a successful farm.

A farmer must combine knowledge of many different occupations to be successful. Explain how a farmer is like:

a scientist must study the chemistry of the soil and make the soil best for the crops

a mechanic must know which machines to use and how they work

a fortune-teller must know which crops people will buy

a weather forecaster must know when to plant and when to harvest

an accountant must keep track of money earned and plan for the next year's expenses

Wednesday | Week 10 | 123

Page 124

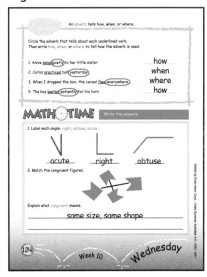

Language Lines — An adverb tells how, when, or where.

Circle the adverb that tells about each underlined verb. Then write *how, when,* or *where* to tell how the adverb is used.

1. Annie *sang* quietly to her little sister.   how
2. Carlos *practiced ball* yesterday.   when
3. When I dropped the box, the cereal *flew* everywhere.   where
4. The boy *waited* patiently for his turn.   how

MATH TIME — Write the answers.

1. Label each angle: right, obtuse, acute.
   acute   right   obtuse

2. Match the congruent figures.

Explain what *congruent* means.
same size, same shape

124 | Week 10 | Wednesday

139

Page 125

Geography

1. How many countries are labeled on this map? **6**
2. Which is larger, Taiwan or Japan? **Japan**
3. Which East Asian capital is the farthest...

east? **Tokyo**
west? **Ulan Bator**
south? **Taipei**
north? **Ulan Bator**

(map showing Mongolia, China, North Korea, South Korea, Japan, Taiwan, Beijing, etc.)

In My Own Words...

Make a list of three questions that you would answer "Yes."

Questions will vary.

Make a list of three questions that you would answer "No."

Thursday   Week 10   125

Page 126

Use *is, are, was,* and *were* correctly.

1. The girls **were** so busy fishing, they forgot the time. "I'm getting hungry," announced Cherrie.
2. Cindy **was** ready for a snack too. "The sandwiches **are** in that sack. There **are** some cookies too," she said.
3. "**Is** there anything to drink?" asked Cherrie.
4. "The juice **is** in the thermos over there," answered Cindy.

MATH TIME   Find the answers.

1. Larry pointed his birdhouse from 3:45 p.m. until 5:00 p.m. How long did he work?   **1 hour, 15 minutes**

2. Clara's new watch is guaranteed for 90 days. About how many months is that?   **3 months**

3. Tasha bought some new clothes. The total of her purchase was $72.27. If she gave the clerk $80, how much money did she get back?   **$7.73**

126   Week 10   Thursday

Page 127

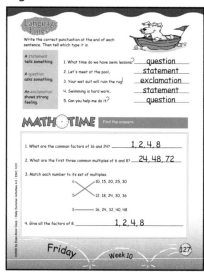

Language Lines

Write the correct punctuation at the end of each sentence. Then tell which type it is.

A *statement* tells something.

A *question* asks something.

An *exclamation* shows strong feeling.

1. What time do we have swim lessons?   **question**
2. Let's meet at the pool.   **statement**
3. Your wet suit will ruin the rug!   **exclamation**
4. Swimming is hard work.   **statement**
5. Can you help me do it?   **question**

MATH TIME   Find the answers.

1. What are the common factors of 16 and 24?   **1, 2, 4, 8**

2. What are the first three common multiples of 6 and 8?   **24, 48, 72**

3. Match each number to its set of multiples.

6 —— 10, 15, 20, 25, 30
5 —— 12, 18, 24, 30, 36
8 —— 16, 24, 32, 40, 48

4. Give all the factors of 8.   **1, 2, 4, 8**

Friday   Week 10   127

Page 128

The Starting Line

Ten students are in the final round of the Spelling Bee. For the newspaper photo, they lined up in order from tallest to shortest. Name the spellers in the photograph.

1. Amber is standing next to Carlos.
2. Hoa is just taller than Jamal, who is standing next to Maria, who is shorter.
3. Carlos is the tallest person.
4. Raul is taller than Maria, and they are both taller than Victor.
5. No one is standing between Raul (the taller) and Yasmin.
6. No one is standing between Fran and Amber.
7. Yasmin is shorter than Olga, who is just shorter than Fran.
8. Olga is taller than Raul, who is taller than Hoa. They are all taller than Maria.

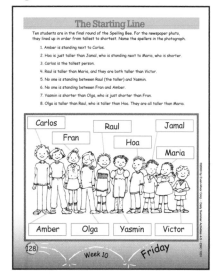

Carlos   Fran   Raul   Hoa   Jamal   Maria

Amber   Olga   Yasmin   Victor

128   Week 10   Friday

Multiplication Strategies

Times 0	0 Times a number is always 0.
Times 1	Times 1 equals the number.
Times 2	Times 2 is double the number.
Times 3	Times 3 is the number tripled. Double the number and add one more group.
Times 4	Times 4 is double Times 2. Times 4 = Times 2 + Times 2. Double the number and double again.
Times 5	Times 5 is like counting nickels. Times 5 is half of Times 10. Times 5 = Times 10 ÷ 2.
Times 6	Times 6 is double Times 3. Times 6 = Times 3 + Times 3. Times 6 = Times 5 + Times 1.
Times 7	Turn Times 7 into smaller multiplication facts: Times 7 = Times 5 + Times 2.
Times 8	Times 8 is double Times 4. Times 8 = Times 4 + Times 4.
Times 9	See Times 9. Think Times 10. Think Times 10 and subtract one group. Times 9 = Times 10 – Times 1.
Times 10	Times 10 increases a number tenfold. Put a 0 in the ones place to increase its value.
Times 11	Single-digit factors Times 11 make double-digit products. (3 × 11 = 33) Times 11 is one group more than Times 10. Times 11 = Times 10 + Times 1.
Times 12	Times 12 = Times 10 + Times 2. Times 12 = Times 6 + Times 6.

Cursive Handwriting

Aa   Bb   Cc   Dd

Ee   Ff   Gg   Hh

Ii   Jj   Kk   Ll

Mm   Nn   Oo   Pp

Qq   Rr   Ss   Tt

Uu   Vv   Ww   Xx

Yy   Zz